Stonehenge

Julian Richards

CONTENTS

Tour of Stonehenge

Site Overview

Stonehenge sits within an area of grassland, bordered to the south by the A303, the main route from London to the South West. This setting has recently been much improved by the removal of the old A344, a major road which ran just north of Stonehenge. Visitors now approach from the west and, once at Stonehenge, follow a route that circles clockwise around the monument, allowing views of all parts of the site that survive above ground.

Although Stonehenge today is a hugely impressive ruin, it would have looked very different when first built. The circular ditch and bank, the earliest elements of the monument, were formed of the chalk that underlies the site and, when first dug out and built about 3000 BC, would have been gleaming white. Also from this early stage of Stonehenge's construction is a circle of large pits known as the Aubrey Holes which lie close to the inner edge of the bank. They originally held upright timbers or small stones and some are now indicated on the ground with metal and stone markers. Surrounding the central stones, but unmarked on the ground, are two circles of smaller pits known as the Y holes and the Z holes.

The most visible elements of Stonehenge are the stones themselves. Some are small, unshaped or broken, others massive, finely worked and intact. The stones of the central cluster, brought to the site about 2500 BC, are arranged in a series of circular and horseshoe-shaped structures. Other stones, near the inner edge of the bank, and in the entrance to the earthwork enclosure, had companions that have now vanished.

The arrival of the stones marked a radical change in the appearance of Stonehenge and the huge sarsens, once in place, remained there. But the smaller bluestones were rearranged in different ways and some were removed or destroyed. The position of the stones today reflects only the last of these settings, completed by about 2200 BC and restored in the 20th century.

Facing page: The great sarsen circle: the north-east section from inside Stonehenge

Below: Drawing of Stonehenge as it appears today

1. Earthwork bank
2. Ditch
3. Aubrey Hole markers
4. Avenue
5. Heel Stone
6. Partner to Heel Stone marker
7. Slaughter Stone
8. Station Stones
9. Station Stone markers
10. South 'Barrow'
11. North 'Barrow'
12. Sarsen circle
13. Bluestone circle
14. Horseshoe of trilithons
15. Bluestone horseshoe

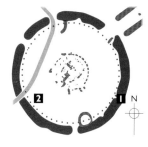

Above right: The ditch and
bank of the enclosure, their
profile softened by 5,000
years of erosion

Above: Bones of a raven
found in the ditch, where
the remains of both wild
and domestic animals have
been found

Below: This ox jawbone, found
in the ditch at Stonehenge,
gave a radiocarbon date
several hundred years earlier
than the ditch itself. This bone
probably had special
significance and may have
been buried as an offering

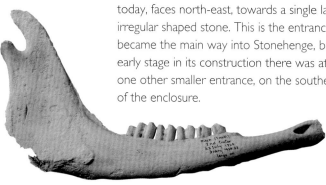

⬛ EARTHWORK ENCLOSURE

Approaching Stonehenge, it is easy to focus on the
stones themselves and ignore the low earthworks
of the ditch and bank that surround them. These
earthworks, dug into the white chalk and originally
far more prominent, represent the first Stonehenge,
constructed shortly after 3000 BC in the period
known as the Neolithic or New Stone Age.

This first Stonehenge was a roughly circular
enclosure of about 110m (360ft) in diameter,
defined by a ditch, an inner bank made of the
chalk excavated from the ditch and, in places, a
small outer bank known as a counterscarp. There
were at least two entrances formed by breaks in
the ditch and bank. One of these, still clearly visible
today, faces north-east, towards a single large
irregular shaped stone. This is the entrance that
became the main way into Stonehenge, but at this
early stage in its construction there was at least
one other smaller entrance, on the southern side
of the enclosure.

When archaeologist Colonel William Hawley
(1851–1941) excavated much of the eastern side of
Stonehenge in the 1920s, he found the silted-up
ditch to be very irregular, varying considerably in
width, depth and shape. He likened it to 'a string
of badly-made sausages'. These early excavations
also show that the ditch, when almost full of
centuries of silt and soil, was 'recut' in about
2450 BC, the silts partly dug out to redefine the
original enclosure.

The ditch was originally dug using picks of red
deer antler, with the chalk to build the banks most
probably moved in baskets or skins. Fragments of
these antler picks, thrown away or perhaps
deliberately left on the ditch floor, have been
radiocarbon dated to between 3000 and 2920 BC
(see feature opposite). But other, older bones
were also found on the ditch floor. In the ends of
some of the short segments of ditch, cattle bones,
jaws and a skull had been carefully placed. When
dated they turned out to be much older than the
ditch, perhaps by as much as 300 years. These old
bones must have been very special, perhaps
offerings of some kind, left by the builders to mark
the foundation of the new temple of Stonehenge.

In this, its first form, Stonehenge is not a proper 'henge' as defined by archaeologists, as a henge has its bank outside its ditch. It is more like earlier sites known as causewayed enclosures, which have irregularly dug ditches with many entrances. These were used in a variety of ways, as meeting places for feasting, some for defence and even as special places where human corpses were exposed to become skeletons before burial. The closest example, known as Robin Hood's Ball, lies about 2.5 miles (4km) to the north-west (see page 28).

❷ AUBREY HOLES

Although we can be certain about when the enclosure was built, it is less certain which of Stonehenge's other features were constructed at this time. One strong possibility is the circle of 56 large circular pits, spaced between 4m and 5m (13ft and 16ft) apart, that lies just inside the inner edge of the bank. These pits are known as the Aubrey Holes after their original discoverer, the 17th-century antiquary John Aubrey (1626–97), who was one of the first to make systematic observations of Stonehenge.

Aubrey Holes were first excavated by Hawley in the early 1920s, since when there has been

much discussion about what, if anything, stood in them. Hawley originally suggested that they had held small stone pillars, but then revised this to large timber posts. What is more certain is that the holes, at some time early in their history, were places of burial. Cremated human bones were found in the filling of the Aubrey Holes and also in the bank and the ditch (which was by this time partly filled in). The only dated cremation from an Aubrey Hole is from about 3000 BC so, during its early life, Stonehenge was a cemetery, a place where the remains of the dead could be

Left: Portrait of John Aubrey by William Faithorne, 1666. Aubrey was a Wiltshire-born antiquary who produced the first plan of Stonehenge to identify the circle of pits around the inner edge of the bank, now known as Aubrey Holes

Dating Stonehenge

Before written history it is necessary to depend on archaeology to provide the evidence for the date of events or structures. Distinctive objects – pottery, flint tools or metalwork – can provide a broad indication of date but only science, in particular radiocarbon dating, can provide more precision.

All living things contain carbon, including a naturally radioactive form of carbon. When something dies, the radioactivity in this carbon decays gradually over time. Radiocarbon dating measures the amount of radioactive carbon remaining in an archaeological sample, for example bone, antler or charcoal. When calibrated against the radiocarbon content of tree rings with a known age, this can give a very precise date.

At Stonehenge, not all the individual events and structures can be dated, but radiocarbon dates were obtained for the antler picks used to dig the ditch and for a number of animal bones found at the bottom of the ditch.

These showed, with 95 per cent probability, that the first stage of the monument was constructed between 3000 and 2920 BC and that some of the animal bones were several hundred years older. Other carbon samples from the site have given dates for the early sarsen stone settings of about 2500 BC and for the final bluestone settings of about 2200 BC. Surprisingly, excavations carried out in 2008 within the stone circles produced dates ranging from the Mesolithic (Middle Stone Age), about 8000 BC, to Roman and later. These show that the site and the area around it were being used both long before and long after its main period of construction and use.

Above: A deer antler pick (left) and rake (right) used to dig the ditch, radiocarbon dated to between 3000 and 2920 BC

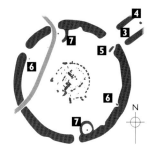

Above right: In winter, snow picks out the ditches of the Avenue in the approach to Stonehenge

Above: A long delicate bone pin found buried with a cremation in one of the Aubrey Holes. The pin may have fastened a shroud around the body before cremation

laid to rest. The cremated bones from Hawley's excavations, reburied in 1935 in an empty Aubrey Hole, were re-excavated in 2008. They appear to be the remains of about 60 individuals, a mixture of men, women and some children, the majority dating from the three centuries after the ditch was first dug. This latest excavation suggested that the chalk on the base of the pit may have been crushed by a heavy object. This has reopened the debate about whether or not the Aubrey Holes originally contained stones, perhaps some of the bluestone pillars.

🔳 AVENUE

The twin parallel banks and ditches of the Avenue can be seen running out straight across the grass field from the main north-easterly entrance of the Stonehenge enclosure. The Avenue marks a route which starts at a newly discovered henge on the bank of the river Avon at West Amesbury, over 1.5 miles (2.5km) away to the south-east. From here it curves up across the A303, crosses the ridge to the east and runs down into a shallow valley where it makes an abrupt turn. The final section then runs straight for a distance of over 500m (550yd) up to the entrance of the Stonehenge enclosure.

The low earthworks of this final section are just visible, particularly in low sunlight or snowy conditions. Recent excavations have shown that they follow the line of natural geological features – gullies and ridges in the surface of the chalk, formed at the end of the last ice age, but which could have been visible as shallow surface hollows to the builders of Stonehenge.

The Avenue was probably constructed in about 2300 BC, more than a century after the great central stone structures had been built. It is interpreted as a ceremonial approach to Stonehenge from the river Avon.

4 HEEL STONE

Immediately outside the entrance to the earthwork enclosure and within the line of the Avenue stands the Heel Stone, or 'Friar's Heel' to give it its older name. This is a huge unshaped boulder of sarsen, a hard reddish sandstone. Most of the sarsens at Stonehenge are thought to have been transported from the Marlborough Downs to the north, but the Heel Stone may have always been here and was simply raised upright.

Today the Heel Stone stands in isolation, surrounded by a small circular ditch, but the hole for another stone was discovered next to it in the roadside verge in 1979. There are two interpretations for this newly discovered hole. It may have held the Heel Stone which was subsequently moved to the position it now stands in. Or there may have been a pair to the Heel Stone, two upright sarsens standing just outside the entrance to the enclosure.

5 SLAUGHTER STONE

In the main entrance to the Stonehenge enclosure lies another large sarsen, the Slaughter Stone, its gruesome name a product of over-active Victorian imagination. It originally stood upright and, like the Heel Stone, was flanked by additional stones that are now missing. The surviving stone now lies horizontally, and shallow depressions on its surface collect rainwater which reacts with iron in the stone and turns a rusty red. This was thought to be evidence of sacrifice – a relic of ancient blood spilt on a stone altar – hence the stone's lurid but highly inaccurate name.

6 STATION STONES AND 7 NORTH AND SOUTH 'BARROWS'

As the path continues around the perimeter of the enclosure, it passes a small sarsen stone close to the inner edge of the bank. This is one of four, known as the Station Stones, that originally stood on roughly the same line as the Aubrey Holes. Of the four, two still survive: one upright, the other fallen, with both showing some signs of having been shaped. The two missing stones were each surrounded by a roughly circular ditch, creating the appearance of low mounds that became known as the North and South 'Barrows'. Despite this name they are not burial mounds.

The Station Stones were most probably put in place at the same time that the central sarsen stones were raised, and their precise position was very carefully calculated. They mark the corners of a perfect rectangle with its central point in the exact centre of the monument. The reason for this is uncertain, although it has been suggested that the Station Stones were survey markers for the original builders.

Above: The Heel Stone, an unshaped sarsen standing within the Avenue

Below: The Slaughter Stone, seen here in the foreground with its puddles of rusty red rainwater, was never a sacrificial altar, but simply a fallen upright in the entrance to the enclosure

The Sarsen Stones and Bluestones

In the form of its ditch and the animal bones that were carefully placed there, the first Stonehenge was not so different from other enclosures of a similar date. Even cremated human bones have been found at other sites of this time. What made Stonehenge so unusual is what happened next. The arrival of the stones in about 2500 BC transformed Stonehenge from something simple and quite ordinary into something unique and quite extraordinary.

Looking at the central stones, it is immediately obvious that they fall into two different groups in terms of their size. Many of them are very large, including the uprights closest to the path and, further in towards the centre, the pairs of even taller uprights that support horizontal lintels. Others, nestled among the larger stones, are much smaller, some less than the height of an adult. These two groups of stones are quite different, both in their size and in the type of raw material from which they are formed.

The largest stones, some of which weigh over 35 tonnes, are known as sarsens. Sarsen is a type of extremely hard sandstone, small boulders of which can be found in the area around Stonehenge. But for larger sarsens the closest consistent source lies more than 19 miles (30km) to the north of Stonehenge, on the Marlborough Downs in north Wiltshire. Here massive stones can still be seen half-buried in the bottoms of valleys, although many have been broken up for building material or cleared away to make cultivation easier.

The smaller stones at Stonehenge are known collectively as bluestones, although this group includes a variety of different types of rock. What unites them is their source: in the Preseli Hills of Wales, over 150 miles (240km) to the west of Stonehenge. There is no doubt about their origin: the mineral composition of stones from Stonehenge can be matched precisely with samples from Preseli.

It is difficult to explain the peculiar mixture of rock types within the bluestones, but perhaps it represents not simply a collection of building materials, but the components of an existing stone circle that stood in Wales before being uprooted and brought to Stonehenge. There were originally at least 80 bluestones at Stonehenge, some weighing up to three tonnes.

So how did both types of stone get to Salisbury Plain? The sarsens are bigger but are found closer to Stonehenge, and experiments have shown that stones this size can be dragged on a simple wooden sledge by a team of about 200 people. To drag a stone from the Marlborough Downs to Stonehenge, using a route that, wherever possible, avoided steep slopes, would take about 12 days.

There have been suggestions that the bluestones were found lying on Salisbury Plain where they had been carried by the movement of glaciers during the last ice age. But there is no geological evidence to support this idea and it is now generally accepted that it was human rather than glacial transport that moved them. Although the bluestones are smaller, they had much further to travel and their route is still open to debate. The first part of their journey would have been by land but water transport may also have been important. The river Avon, which flows close to Stonehenge, is often suggested as forming the final part of the bluestones' journey from Wales.

Below left: Bluestone outcrops in the Preseli Hills in Wales
Below right: Natural sarsens can still be found on the Marlborough Downs
Bottom: Map showing the possible routes by which the bluestones (yellow) and the sarsen stones (purple) may have been transported to Stonehenge

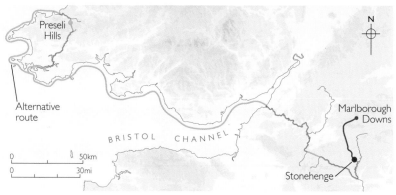

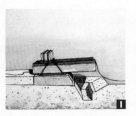

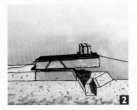

Shaping and Raising the Stones

Having moved their building materials to Stonehenge, how did our prehistoric ancestors shape and erect the stones?

Although Stonehenge was built during a time when stone tools were gradually being replaced by those of copper and bronze, these new metals were too soft to have been used to shape hard stone. Both sarsen and bluestone could only have been shaped using stone tools – round sarsen balls known as mauls or hammerstones. Many have been found at Stonehenge, from the size of an orange to some as big as footballs. Huge quantities of stone working debris suggest that the main sarsen working area lay on the slope just to the north of the enclosure.

Once shaped, the stones intended as uprights could be raised. Holes were dug into the chalk, the depth of each one calculated in order to level up the tops of the stones. Excavation has shown that most of the holes that hold upright stones have one straight side and one that slopes. The stone would have been slid into the hole to rest at an angle against the sloping side.

Experiments have shown that this can be done by balancing the stone on a ramp with its end poised over the hole **1**. Smaller stones can then be used to overbalance, pivot on the solid end of the ramp **2** and drop into the hole **3**. The stone is then hauled upright against the vertical face using ropes of hide or vegetable fibre **4**. Finally the hole is backfilled with chalk, fragments of stone, bits of broken deer antler picks and mauls, all rammed down firmly to hold the stone in place.

There are several theories as to how the lintels were raised into position. A sloping ramp of earth or timber may have been used but alternatively the lintels could have been lifted on a platform of interlocking timbers. Each end of the lintel would have been raised in turn using levers. As each end was levered up, supporting timbers would have been inserted and the stone rose as the platform grew in height. Either of these methods is possible and neither would have left any trace for archaeologists to find.

Above: Diagrams showing one possible way to raise the lintel stones by using wooden levers to lift each end of the lintel in turn, and supporting it on a wooden platform that was built up around both uprights (top). When the platform was the same height as the uprights, the lintel could have been levered into place (bottom)
Left: The carefully worked surface of an upright stone in the sarsen circle
Below: A collection of flint and sarsen hammerstones found at Stonehenge

The Stone Settings

Using sarsen and bluestone the builders of Stonehenge created remarkable and unique structures. At most stone circles built at this time in prehistory, the blocks of stone were left in their natural, rough state and simply raised upright, but at Stonehenge they were treated differently. The sarsens within the central settings have been carefully trimmed, sometimes to produce sharply defined rectangular blocks, and have also been shaped to produce simple joints that lock the stones tightly together. Some of the bluestones

Below: The circles of sarsens and bluestones, showing the contrasting sizes of the two different types of stone

also show evidence of shaping and jointing, although in their final setting they all seem to have been freestanding.

What can be seen today are the ruins of the stone settings that were constructed over several centuries. Once in place about 2500 BC, the huge sarsens do not appear to have been moved but, in contrast, the smaller bluestones, also introduced at this time, may subsequently have been rearranged several times. There are four concentric settings, two circles and two of horseshoe shape, all of which, even after more than 4,000 years of decay, can still be recognized today.

8 SARSEN CIRCLE

The outermost setting, if completed, was a circle of 30 upright sarsens, capped by horizontal lintel stones, all carefully shaped. Of these 30 uprights only 17 still stand while only six of the lintels are still in place, leaving the best preserved section on the north-eastern side facing the entrance to the enclosure. The surviving uprights are closely spaced with gaps of less than 1.5m (5ft) between the individual stones. There is a slightly wider gap between the stones that most directly face the main entrance.

The uprights and the lintels are locked together by means of a joint more commonly used in woodworking: the mortise and tenon. A protruding peg, or tenon, on the top of each upright, fits into a corresponding hole, or mortise, hollowed out of the underside of the lintel. The ends of the lintels are locked together by tongue and groove joints (also derived from carpentry) where a vertical tongue fits into a corresponding vertical groove. The sophistication of this part of the structure is increased by the shaping of the horizontal lintels: these are not straight sided as might be expected but gently curved on both inner and outer faces. If this outer circle – now much ruined – was ever complete (see page 12), then its lintels would have formed a smooth ring of stone suspended high and perfectly level above the ground.

9 BLUESTONE CIRCLE

Inside and concentric with these sarsens lay a circular setting of as many as 60 small, upright bluestones. These are of a variety of Preseli stones including dolerites, rhyolites and ash stones with the largest slabs flanking a wider gap that marks the entrance alignment. The majority of these bluestones show no signs of having been worked or shaped but within this circle there are two finely worked stones with mortise holes. These were clearly shaped and used as horizontal lintels on miniature bluestone trilithons before being reused as upright pillars. This circle, the final arrangement of these smaller stones, is now very fragmentary, with evidence of some stones being deliberately broken up and removed from site.

Top: Diagram showing the joints used on the sarsen circle, with a mortise and tenon joint locking the uprights to the lintels and a tongue and groove joint locking the lintels together end-to-end

Above: The top of one of the sarsens on the north-east side of Stonehenge – the protruding tenons can still be clearly seen

Below: A finely shaped bluestone lintel discovered during excavation in 1954

Was Stonehenge Completed?

Surviving sections of the sarsen circle suggest that it was intended to have 30 uprights capped with 30 horizontal lintels, together forming a complete and perfect circle. But in its ruined state, as well as fallen and broken stones, there are many completely missing, particularly to the south-west, in marked contrast to the more complete north-eastern side. In addition there is the problem of Stone 11, an upright sarsen on the south side. It is in the correct position on the line of the circle, but is far too small to have supported a lintel with its full-sized neighbours. This and the missing stones have been suggested as evidence that Stonehenge was never finished. A more likely explanation is that more effort was expended in completing what was seen as being the more important, more 'public' side of Stonehenge, the one that would be seen from the entrance and the Avenue, leaving the 'rear' less carefully constructed.

Above: A view of Stonehenge *from the south with Stone* *11, the problem stone,* *leaning at a slight angle in* *the centre right foreground*

ⅿ SARSEN TRILITHONS

Moving inwards, the next setting was the most impressive: a horseshoe of five massive sarsen trilithons (from the Greek for 'three stones'). Each trilithon consisted of two huge and closely spaced uprights and an equally huge horizontal lintel. These stones were again locked together with mortise and tenon joints. Three complete trilithons still stand (although the one closest to the tarmac path fell in 1797 and was re-erected in 1958). Among their uprights are the biggest individual stones at Stonehenge, weighing well over 35 tonnes. When first found on the Marlborough Downs in north Wiltshire, before they were so carefully shaped, the rough stones must have weighed considerably more.

This sarsen horseshoe is an extremely sophisticated structure as the individual trilithons were originally graded in height, with the tallest, known as the Great Trilithon, standing at the closed end of the horseshoe. Only one stone of this magnificent structure still stands, one of the tallest standing stones in Britain, over 7.3m (24ft) high. The large tenon which protrudes from the top of this stone is clearly visible. Each pair of trilithon uprights shows evidence of 'pairing' with one stone deliberately much smoother and more carefully shaped than the other. Some of these uprights were decorated with shallow carvings of daggers and axes made over 700 years after they were raised (see page 41).

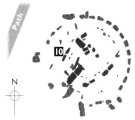

Left: *A great sarsen stone trilithon – two massive uprights capped by a horizontal lintel – one of five that stood at Stonehenge*

Facing page: *The setting midwinter sun sends its rays into the centre of Stonehenge*

Right: *Midsummer dawn with the sun rising in the north-east over the Heel Stone*

Below: *Midwinter sunset at Maes Howe, a Neolithic chambered tomb on Orkney. At midwinter, the setting sun shines down the passage to illuminate the burial chamber*

The Alignment of Stonehenge

Stonehenge has an 'axis' – an alignment that runs north-east to south-west, up the final straight section of the Avenue and through the enclosure entrance.

Within the central stones this alignment runs through the open ends of the horseshoes of sarsen and bluestone to where the Altar Stone lies at the base of the Great Trilithon.

This axis was carefully chosen because it reflects important events in the annual movement of the sun. At Stonehenge on the summer solstice, the longest day of the year, about 21 June in the modern calendar, the sun rises behind the Heel Stone in the north-east part of the horizon and its first rays shine into the heart of Stonehenge. This alignment is deliberate; it is shared with many other henges – temples of earth and wood – that were built around the same time. Close to Stonehenge there are two good examples, Coneybury to the south-east and Woodhenge to the north-east. But an alignment

that marks a midsummer event in one direction can also point to a midwinter event in the opposite.

Because of the way the sun moves through the sky during the course of the year, the sunset at the winter solstice, the shortest day of the year, occurs on exactly the opposite side of the horizon from the midsummer sunrise. Observers at Stonehenge at the winter solstice (about 21 December), standing in the enclosure entrance and facing the centre of the stones, can watch the sun set in the south-west part of the horizon. When the Great Trilithon stood intact the effect would have been dramatic, the setting sun dropping rapidly down the narrow gap between the two upright stones.

So the alignment of Stonehenge works for both the summer solstice and for the one that happens in winter. But there is increasing evidence from other Neolithic sites such as Newgrange in Ireland and Maes Howe in Orkney, as well as closer by at Durrington Walls, that the winter was the more significant. At Durrington, there is evidence for feasting and celebration at just this time of year.

Right: *At midwinter (left) the sun sets in the south-west part of the sky. At midsummer (right), the sun rises in the north-east. Stonehenge is aligned with both solstices, six months and 180 degrees apart*

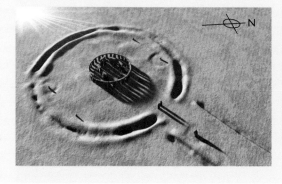

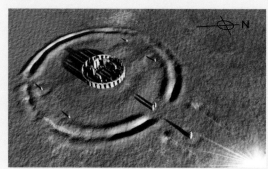

11 BLUESTONE HORSESHOE

The innermost setting is another horseshoe, this time of bluestones, but here almost all of spotted dolerite, the most attractive of the Preseli stones. This horseshoe arrangement may originally have been an oval with some stones later removed to create the present setting. In its original state there were 19 stones, tall pillars in contrast to the short, often slab-like stones of the bluestone circle. Many of these pillars were elegantly shaped including one with a vertical groove worked down its entire length and, like the sarsen trilithons, they rise in height towards the back of the horseshoe. Some bear evidence that they were once capped with protruding tenons suggesting that they supported lintels, although not where they stand today.

12 ALTAR STONE

Finally, at the closed end of the innermost horseshoe, in the shadow of the tallest trilithon and now partly buried beneath both its fallen and broken upright and its massive lintel, lies a stone known as the Altar Stone. This is the largest of the non-sarsen stones, a broken slab of greenish sandstone from south Wales. Unlike the other Welsh stones it is not from the Preseli Hills, recent analysis suggesting that it comes from the area of the Brecon Beacons. As the wreckage of the Great Trilithon has never been moved it is uncertain whether the Altar Stone originally lay flat as an altar-like slab or stood upright.

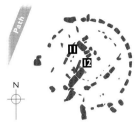

Top: An elegantly grooved stone in the bluestone horseshoe, possibly intended to be jointed to a similar stone with a corresponding tongue. This shaping suggests that the stone was relocated here after having been used previously in some other arrangement, perhaps elsewhere

Bottom left: The Altar Stone exposed during excavations in the 1950s. Today it remains partly buried beneath the fallen stones of the Great Trilithon

Bottom right: Shaped pillars of the bluestone horseshoe stand in front of the remaining upright of the Great Trilithon

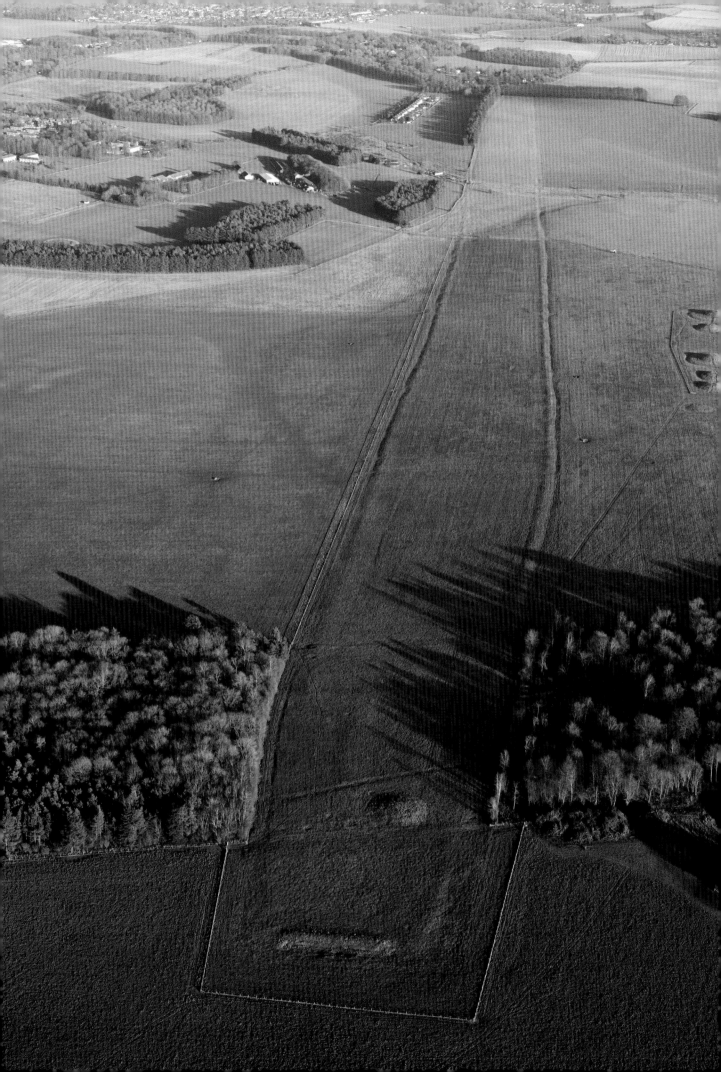

Tour of the Stonehenge Landscape

Overview

Stonehenge lies at the centre of a landscape so rich in prehistoric remains that it is classed as a World Heritage Site. There are burial mounds (long barrows) and elongated earthwork enclosures (cursus monuments) that date from the time before Stonehenge. From the time of building Stonehenge there are other temples (henges) and, from the centuries after building at Stonehenge had ceased, hundreds of Bronze Age burial mounds (round barrows) were built on surrounding hilltops and valley sides. These monuments, all concerned with burial and ceremony, have been recognized for centuries. But they have now been joined by traces of everyday prehistoric life. Aerial photography has revealed traces of small farmsteads, boundary ditches, fields and trackways. Artefacts collected from the surface of ploughed fields ('fieldwalking') provide evidence of both ancient industry and of the places where people lived. The excavations that followed these discoveries have provided detailed glimpses of life in prehistoric times and have shown us how this landscape developed through time.

Although there is open access to much of the landscape surrounding Stonehenge some important monuments are on private land and are not accessible to the public (see page 28).

Before Stonehenge

Before even the first simple earthwork Stonehenge was built, this particular part of Salisbury Plain was clearly important. Evidence for burial and ritual, if not for everyday life, comes from long barrows and cursus monuments, built 500 years previously. But in much earlier times Mesolithic (Middle Stone Age) hunters lived in the valley of the nearby river Avon, rich in wild foods from fish, deer and giant wild cattle to nuts and berries. These people from this remote time also built some unique and largely unexplained structures close to where Stonehenge was to stand thousands of years later.

MESOLITHIC POSTHOLES

In 1966, when the first car park was built at Stonehenge, three large pits were discovered dug into the chalk (a further one was found during building work in 1989). Their positions are to be marked on the ground with wooden and metal markers. All showed evidence that they had originally held large timber posts of about 75cm (30in) in diameter. The wood for the posts was pine – an unusual tree to be found on chalk soils – but the date of the posts was even more unexpected. Radiocarbon dating showed that they were raised during the Mesolithic period, between

Above: The Mesolithic landscape was rich in wild foods: from nuts and berries to animals like red deer
Left: The eastern portion of Stonehenge's Avenue revealed by aerial photography: the lines of the banks show up clearly as parallel crop marks in this 1976 photograph

Facing page: A view along the Neolithic Stonehenge Cursus looking east, with the Bronze Age Cursus Barrows visible to the right

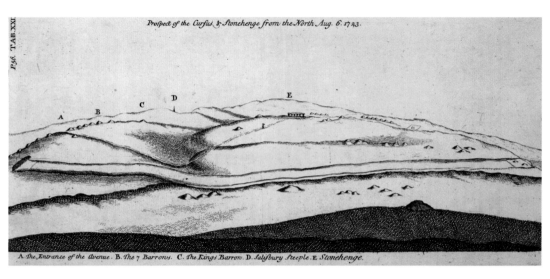

Prospect of the Cursus & Stonehenge from the North. Aug. 6. 1723.

A. The Entrance of the Avenue. B. The 7 Barrows. C. The Kings Barrow. D. Salisbury Steeple. E. Stonehenge.

Above: A Neolithic antler pick found in the ditch of the Stonehenge Cursus

Above right: In the early 18th century the antiquary William Stukeley was able to record the entire Stonehenge Cursus, which survived as an earthwork

Below: A view of the Winterbourne Stoke Crossroads Long Barrow from the north-east, before the road improvements carried out in 2013

8500 and 7000 BC. This was not long after the end of the last ice age when Britain was still connected to mainland Europe. As sea levels rose in the warming climate, trees grew: initially pine and hazel. Within this forest bands of hunters and gatherers lived on wild foods. It was these people who raised the posts, unique structures, more than 9,000 years old, and perhaps best interpreted as poles of the kind found on Native North American sites, commonly known as totem poles. By the time that work started nearby on building Stonehenge more than 4,000 years later, there can have been nothing more than shallow hollows on the ground to mark where these enigmatic posts once stood.

STONEHENGE CURSUS

Built centuries before the first Stonehenge was the unusual monument known as the Stonehenge Cursus. This is an elongated earthwork enclosure with a ditch and bank that defines an area more than 100m (330ft) wide and 1.7 miles (2.7km) long. It runs east–west across the downland to the north of Stonehenge, crossing a shallow valley towards its central part. The ditches on its long sides are small, little over 1m (3ft) deep, and, where investigated, sometimes quite irregularly dug. Both ends appear to have been defined by much larger ditches and correspondingly bigger banks. Its eastern end stops just short of a levelled Neolithic long barrow while a round barrow stands within its western terminal.

It was first noted by the early 18th-century antiquary William Stukeley (1687–1765), who decided that it was Roman in date and had been built for racing chariots or horses (hence the names

he gave it, Cursus or Hippodrome, both classical words for racetracks). He was wrong about the date: it was built in the early Neolithic period in about 3400 BC, when many long barrows were also built, but its function still remains uncertain. The few finds from the ditches suggest that it may have been laid out as a special or sacred space, perhaps for processions or as a barrier across the landscape. The entire length of the Stonehenge Cursus lies on National Trust open access land. The gap through Fargo Plantation marks the width of the Stonehenge Cursus at this, its western end, where the earthworks have been partially reconstructed.

WINTERBOURNE STOKE CROSSROADS LONG BARROW

The long barrow at Winterbourne Stoke Crossroads, which formed the focus for a later Bronze Age round barrow cemetery, has a mound over 80m (262ft) long and over 25m (82ft) wide. Flanking it are traces of the quarry ditches that supplied material for its construction. Human remains were discovered in the 1860s underneath the wider and higher north-eastern end of the mound. These remains have recently been radiocarbon dated and show that the long barrow was built in about 3500 BC.

Long barrows are ancestral tombs containing groups of burials that may lie within a wooden or stone structure: a symbolic house for the dead. Spectacular when first built, its white chalk mound highly visible in the landscape, this long barrow was raised not simply to contain bones, but as a way of establishing a claim to the land on which it stood.

At the Time of Stonehenge

Stonehenge should not be seen as a monument that sat in splendid isolation. At the time it was built, its Avenue provided a physical link out into the wider landscape and, through the river Avon, a link to other sites, both near at hand and within the wider world. Within Stonehenge's landscape lie other monuments, great and small, built at this time of great change, together with the first evidence of the very people who perhaps moved and raised the stones.

DURRINGTON WALLS

In about 2500 BC, when the great stones were being brought to Stonehenge, other henges – enclosures of chalk and timber – were being built within the surrounding landscape. The greatest of these was Durrington Walls, a massive enclosure over 470m (500yd) in diameter that lies within a broad hollow on the west bank of the river Avon nearly 2 miles (3km) north-east of Stonehenge. Durrington is a more traditional henge, with a huge bank lying outside an equally massive ditch, but despite its size it is difficult to see from ground level.

There are four entrances to the enclosure, the most obvious one pointing south-east down towards the river. Excavations carried out between 1966 and 1968 on the line of the road that cuts through the henge revealed the ditch to be over 6m (20ft) deep and 13m (43ft) wide. It also uncovered the remains of two complex timber structures, the Northern Circle and the larger Southern Circle, 23m (75ft) in diameter. Each had multiple concentric settings of large timbers and produced quantities of pottery, animal bones and flint tools.

More recent excavations, from 2004 onwards, have shown that, like Stonehenge, Durrington has an avenue: a gravelled pathway which runs from the Southern Circle through the south-eastern entrance and down to the river Avon. This avenue also has a solstice alignment, marking sunset at midsummer and sunrise at midwinter. Close by – and preserved under the huge henge bank – the remains of Neolithic houses were discovered, the first to have been found in southern Britain. Recent research has shown that at many henges the construction of the enclosure may be the last

Above: Many everyday items were found during excavations at Durrington Walls. These included a pot in the distinctive style known as 'Grooved Ware', often associated with Neolithic henge monuments (top – now in the Salisbury and South Wiltshire Museum), a shale bead (middle) and a bone pin (bottom)

The River Avon in Prehistory

It is easy to regard rivers as barriers, rather than as routeways. Today, when water comes from a tap, its source is often forgotten. But to the prehistoric people who lived in the Stonehenge area the river and its valley were vital. It was a source of water for drinking both for people and for domesticated animals and it also supplied food. Edible plants grew in the damper soils; fish – trout and salmon – could be caught, while deer and other wild animals could be hunted as they came to drink. Otters and beavers, valued for their fur, swam in the river's clear waters.

But beyond these practical uses, and the possibility that its waters were used to transport the bluestones on the last stage of their journey from Wales, the river may have had a more spiritual importance. Precious objects deposited in rivers and lakes show that prehistoric people may have regarded their waters as sacred. Some archaeologists have put forward the idea that the river was part of the journey taken by the dead from Durrington to Stonehenge, as both have avenues – physical connections with the flowing waters.

Right: The river Avon was perhaps sacred to the builders of Stonehenge

Right: One of the stone-built Neolithic houses, complete with furniture, at Skara Brae in Orkney

settlement in Orkney where the walls and furniture are made of stone and have therefore survived for over 4,000 years.

Separating the individual houses were fences of wooden stakes against which rubbish had piled up. Huge quantities of animal bone, mostly young pig, suggest large-scale feasting, possibly in midwinter. The discovery of these houses, and the evidence of similar structures from other points around the henge, show that before the enclosure was built there may have been hundreds of houses and perhaps thousands of people living at Durrington. This may be the largest Neolithic settlement in Britain and Ireland, although probably only occupied at certain times of year. So were these the houses of the people who built and used Stonehenge?

Other houses, some larger and surrounded by deep ditches, like smaller henges, were found inside the main enclosure. These lack the evidence of everyday life, of food and cooking, that characterizes most of the houses and may have had a special, possibly ritual function. The timber circles discovered in the 1960s, and recently re-examined

act in what can be a long sequence of use. So here at Durrington evidence suggests that some, if not all, of the houses were built, used and abandoned before the ditch was dug and the bank built.

The houses were small and roughly square, the majority about 5m (17ft) across, with walls of woven hazel covered in daub, and inside a square floor of hard packed chalk, in the centre of which was a hearth. The space between the chalk floor and the outer wall may have been filled with wooden furniture, beds and cupboards. In their layout these houses are almost identical to those of the same date from Skara Brae, a Neolithic

Right: Reconstruction of the Neolithic settlement at Durrington Walls in about 2500 BC, looking west
1 Northern Circle
2 Southern Circle
3 Avenue
4 River Avon
5 Neolithic houses

Life at Durrington Walls

Life at Durrington Walls at the time of building Stonehenge would have been sociable, busy and preoccupied not only with everyday activities, but also with ceremony.

The people lived in their small houses, clustered together but separated from their neighbours by woven wooden fences. In these houses, each large enough to have easily contained a small family, food was prepared around the central hearth, the bones of pigs and cattle indicating a diet rich in meat. Strangely, cereal grain does not seem to have formed a significant part of the diet.

Inside the houses it was dark and smoky, and at night, illuminated by the flames of the fire, the people of Durrington slept beneath skins on low wooden platforms.

This was a place that would have changed, perhaps on a daily basis. People arrived from far away, driving their pigs and cattle, meat for feasts arriving on the hoof, some from far to the north. The daily task may well have been to walk across the low hills to Stonehenge and there shape and raise the great stones.

Left: A reconstruction of a Durrington Walls house, built in 2013
Below: The tip of a flint arrowhead (circled) was found still embedded in this pig bone from Durrington

But this may not have been a permanent home. It is suggested that only part of the year, perhaps the time around the summer and winter solstices, was spent by the banks of the river Avon. When people returned after months away, their houses needed repair, new ones had to be built and, when a house was finally abandoned, a pit had to be dug in which to place all of the rubbish that remained, 'closing' the house for ever.

Above: Finely worked Neolithic flint arrowheads from Durrington Walls

Right: A view from above House 851, one of the Neolithic houses excavated near the eastern entrance to Durrington Walls

1 Stake holes – the traces of small upright timbers, part of wattle walls originally rendered with a chalk cob mixture

2 Floor – made of chalk, beaten flat and worn smooth by human feet

3 Hearth – each house has one in the centre

4 Slots for horizontal wooden boards, the traces of wooden beds, cupboards and other furniture ranged between the walls of the house and the chalk floor

5 Pits – containing pottery, animal bone and flints. They were dug through or outside the house and may have been part of rituals to do with the abandonment of the house

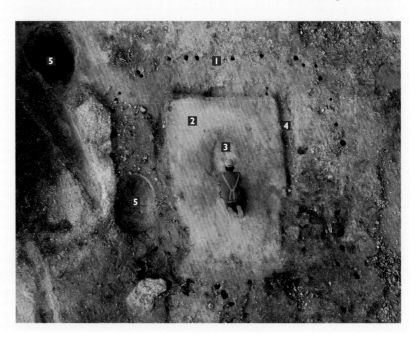

Maud Cunnington

Above: Portrait photograph of Maud Cunnington

Maud Cunnington (1869–1951) was a pioneering archaeologist, famous for her excavation of important prehistoric sites on the chalk of Salisbury Plain.

She started her excavations in 1897 and in the 1920s rediscovered and excavated the Sanctuary (a stone circle near Avebury) and excavated Woodhenge. Both these sites were bought by Maud Cunnington and her husband Benjamin, great-grandson of the antiquarian William Cunnington, and given to the nation. Her excavation techniques and recording were excellent for their time and she promptly analysed and published her findings.

In 1931 she was elected President of the Wiltshire Archaeological Society and in 1948 she was made a CBE for her services to archaeology, the first woman archaeologist to receive this honour.

and reinterpreted, also appear to have had a ritual rather than a practical function. The timbers were also raised before the enclosure was built, but even after they had rotted away, the place where they had stood was still regarded as special and was marked by deposits of animal bone and pottery, more evidence of cooking and feasting.

Durrington Walls is physically linked to Stonehenge by the river Avon and eventually by the Stonehenge Avenue. Its houses, everyday life and timber circles, more of which are found nearby close to Woodhenge, are seen by some as the 'land of the living'. In contrast, Stonehenge, with its cremated human bones and circles of cold stone, is regarded as 'the land of the dead'. Whether or not this is how our Neolithic ancestors regarded their world cannot be proved, but Stonehenge and Durrington are certainly closely linked.

WOODHENGE

To the south of Durrington Walls lies Woodhenge, revealed by aerial photographs taken in 1925 to be a levelled henge. The bank and internal ditch enclose a circular area about 50m (160ft) in diameter with a single entrance facing north-east. Shortly after its discovery the site was excavated by Maud Cunnington. Her work revealed that within the interior lay six concentric circles of pits, varying considerably in size and having originally held large upright oak timbers. Because of the similarity of this plan to that of Stonehenge, this site became known as Woodhenge. Woodhenge did gain some stones, assumed to be sarsens, late in its life, but they were subsequently removed.

From their ground plan, these timber circles (like those at Durrington Walls) are difficult to interpret. The upright timbers may have stood in the open air, either plain or highly decorated. They may have been linked together by horizontal beams to create a wooden version of Stonehenge or may even have been the framework for a huge building.

The finds made in the excavations at Woodhenge include decorated Grooved Ware pottery, flint tools and animal bones, apparently deposited in a very organized way, perhaps at the base of the timber posts before they had rotted away. Each of the timber circles may have had a different meaning or use; some had more pottery, some more animal bone, but perhaps the most disturbing find was a grave that lay in the centre of the site. Now marked on the ground by a small flint cairn, it contained the skeleton of a child aged

Below: The positions of the wooden posts at Woodhenge are now marked with concrete pillars

Left: A reconstruction of Woodhenge as it might have appeared in about 2500 BC. The upright timbers might have been quite simple, or elaborately carved and decorated

Below: Finds from Woodhenge

1 Bone pin

2 Chalk axe (symbolic rather than functional)

3 Fragment of Grooved Ware pottery

4 Flint awl for piercing holes in leather or bone, for example

5 Flint saw

6 Flint 'fabricator' – possibly used as a striker to create sparks for starting fires

about three years old. The excavator suggested that the child's skull had been split, but a more likely explanation is that the individual bones of the skull had not fused together at the time of the child's death.

Woodhenge, which was built in about 2500 BC, is now in the care of English Heritage and has unrestricted visitor access. There is a car park and the excavated postholes are marked by coloured concrete pillars.

CUCKOO STONE

Lying flat in the field immediately west of Woodhenge is a small sarsen boulder known as the Cuckoo (or Cuckold) Stone. Excavations carried out around its present location revealed the shallow hollow in the chalk in which it had originally lain, proving that it was a local stone, not transported to the area like the Stonehenge sarsens. Raised upright at some time late in the Neolithic this small standing stone then became the focus for a number of early Bronze Age cremation burials and may have been a location for other ritual activities, including a later Roman shrine.

Left: The Cuckoo Stone in the field to the west of Woodhenge

After Stonehenge

On every hilltop visible from Stonehenge there are
low grassy mounds. These are round barrows, each
the burial place of someone of wealth and status
in the early part of the Bronze Age. This was the
time, from about 2300 BC until about 1600 BC,
when the building of Stonehenge was largely
complete, with just Y and Z holes to be added
and the trilithons decorated with shallow carvings.

The position of these barrows is quite
deliberate, many of them strung out along the
crests of low ridges where they would have been
most visible. Here they were most able to
advertise the power of the people who lay
beneath them.

The landscape surrounding Stonehenge
contains one of the highest concentrations of
Bronze Age round barrows in the country, their
location influenced by the continuing power of the
stones. The mounds that can be seen today are
just the survivors; originally there were more than
300 within a 2 mile (3km) radius of Stonehenge.
This was a huge attraction for early archaeologists,
with the result that nearly every barrow that can
be seen has been at least partially excavated.

In the early years of the 19th century hundreds
of barrows were excavated by William Cunnington
(1754–1810), a self-taught archaeologist, and

Sir Richard Colt Hoare (1758–1838), his rich
patron. Their methods seem crude by today's
standards, locating the burial, usually placed under
the centre of the mound, by digging a hole straight
down through the barrow mound. But they did
identify different types of barrow, and both
recorded and published their findings in some
detail. They kept the objects they were interested
in, the intact pottery vessels and items of bronze,
amber and gold, but they felt that they could learn
nothing from the human remains and so these
were replaced in the grave. Many of their
magnificent finds can be seen in the Wiltshire
Museum in Devizes and the Salisbury and South
Wiltshire Museum in Salisbury.

STONEHENGE DOWN BARROWS

Within the triangle of land on which Stonehenge
sits are a number of round barrows that can easily
be explored. To the south-west is a group of low
mounds, the survivors of what may have been as
many as seven barrows. The best preserved of
these, close to the A303, is a disc barrow
in which Cunnington found a cremation burial in
the early 19th century. Immediately east of
Stonehenge is a fine bell barrow in which
Cunnington, at a second attempt at excavation,
found a 'large rude sepulchral urn' containing
cremated bones and a pair of bone tweezers.

*Above: Portrait of Sir Richard
Colt Hoare by Henry Edridge*
*Right: Lying just south-west of
Stonehenge itself are the
Stonehenge Down Barrows. In
the distance the Normanton
Down Barrows lie strung out
along a low ridge*

Bronze Age Barrows

Within the Stonehenge landscape the most numerous and spectacular prehistoric monuments are undoubtedly the great groups of round barrows.

These are Bronze Age burial mounds of a wide variety of shapes and sizes. The earliest date from about 2300 BC, the time after Stonehenge had been rebuilt in stone. These barrows continued to be modified and new ones built until about 1500 BC.

Unlike the earlier Neolithic long barrows dating from about 3500 BC that usually contain groups of burials, each Bronze Age round barrow was usually the tomb of an individual. Their remains were either buried or cremated and they were accompanied to the next world with a wide variety of personal possessions, including pottery vessels, tools of stone, bone or bronze, and jewellery of exotic materials such as jet, amber and gold.

Evidence from land snails preserved in the soils buried underneath barrow mounds shows that when they were built the landscape was largely open, well-grazed grassland with few trees. So when first built, the white chalk barrow mounds would have been highly visible in this open landscape, especially when positioned on prominent ridges and hills.

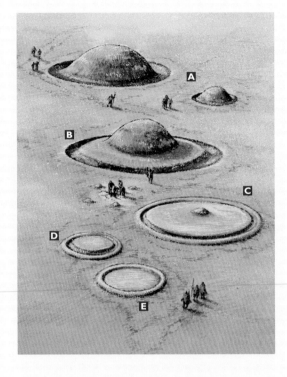

Some barrows were later enlarged or altered and were used for burial over several centuries. The remains that can be seen today are just the last stage in a process of modification and enlargement.

Many of the fine barrow groups that surround Stonehenge lie on National Trust open access land.

Barrow types

A Bowl barrows can vary in size considerably. They have a mound usually surrounded by a ditch

B Bell barrows have a flat or slightly sloping area separating the mound and the surrounding ditch

C Disc barrows have a small mound lying within a flat circular area surrounded by a ditch and an external bank

D Saucer barrows have a low mound surrounded by a ditch and external bank

E Pond barrows, an extremely rare form, have a shallow circular hollow surrounded by a low bank

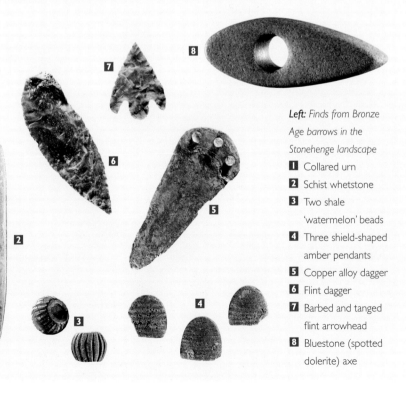

Left: Finds from Bronze Age barrows in the Stonehenge landscape

1 Collared urn
2 Schist whetstone
3 Two shale 'watermelon' beads
4 Three shield-shaped amber pendants
5 Copper alloy dagger
6 Flint dagger
7 Barbed and tanged flint arrowhead
8 Bluestone (spotted dolerite) axe

CURSUS BARROWS

As the name of this group suggests, it lies close to the Stonehenge Cursus, on the crest of a low ridge that runs parallel to its southern bank (see photograph page 16). This position is deliberate: the mounds of the impressive bowl and bell barrows are placed so that they are most prominent and, from Stonehenge, appear silhouetted against the skyline. In 1723 the antiquary William Stukeley investigated some of the barrows in this group, finding cremated human bones and beads of amber and glass that led him to believe he had found the grave of a young woman. In 1803 the barrows were re-examined by Colt Hoare and Cunnington who found more burials and some fine pottery vessels. The Cursus Barrows lie on National Trust open access land.

Above: A portrait of William Cunnington, the great barrow explorer, by Samuel Woodforde, 1808
Right: Aerial photograph of the Winterbourne Stoke Crossroads Bronze Age barrow group, with the Neolithic long barrow at the top right, before the road improvements in 2013
Below: The unexplored mounds of the New King Barrows

OLD AND NEW KING BARROWS

To the east of Stonehenge, a group of large mounds can be seen among the woods that lie on the crest of the closest ridge. These are the King Barrows, Old and New, a group that meanders along the ridge for a distance of over 0.6 miles (1km).

The Old King Barrows, a scattered group of bowl barrows, lie north of the line of the Stonehenge Avenue and include some unusual low examples that appear to have mounds constructed largely of turf. The New King Barrows, a more compact group to the south, contain some of the largest bowl and bell barrows within the

Stonehenge landscape. They are also the only group that was not excavated in the 19th century, only because at that time they were protected by a covering of trees. The only clues about the date and structure of the barrows came from holes torn in the mounds by ancient beech trees felled by a storm in 1990. These suggested that some of the mounds were also of an unusual construction, built largely of turf and capped with chalk from the surrounding ditch.

Although there is no firm evidence for when the New King Barrows were built, their sheer size suggests that they may be of an early date for round barrows, perhaps raised before 2000 BC. Both Old and New King Barrows are visible from a nearby path and there is open access to the New King group.

WINTERBOURNE STOKE CROSSROADS BARROWS

The earliest barrow in this group is a Neolithic long barrow (see page 18) dating from about 3500 BC, the alignment of which was followed, perhaps nearly 1,500 years later, by a line of large bowl and bell barrows. Then, over several hundred more years, as burial fashions changed in the earlier part of the Bronze Age (between about 2000 and

1600 BC), other more elaborate barrow types were added. There are smaller bowl barrows, disc barrows and saucer barrows, their beautiful but shallow forms best appreciated from the air. There are even examples of rare pond barrows.

Almost all the barrows in this group were excavated in the early 19th century, the most notable finds being the remains of two wooden coffins, many decorated pottery vessels and spearheads and daggers of bronze. This extremely well-preserved barrow group has a burial history that may span as much as 2,000 years and contains every type of round barrow to be found in southern England. The Winterbourne Stoke Crossroads Barrows are partly owned by the National Trust and partly privately owned; they can be seen from a nearby path leading from the Fargo Plantation drop-off point.

NORMANTON DOWN BARROWS

The Normanton Down Barrows lie along the crest of a low ridge just to the south of Stonehenge. They were described by Sir Richard Colt Hoare as 'a noble group – diversified in their forms, perfect in their symmetry, and rich in their contents'.

Within the group there are some spectacularly large disc barrows, called 'Druid barrows' by Colt Hoare and his digging collaborator William Cunnington. The finds that they produced, including beads and other personal ornaments, convinced them that disc barrows were the burial places of females.

Colt Hoare's comments about 'rich' barrows were largely due to the finds made in a large mound known as Bush Barrow in 1808. Cunnington had first investigated this mound without result on 11 July of that year but returned in September and found 'the skeleton of a stout and tall man, lying from north to south'. He also found an amazing group of objects, including bronze daggers still with the remains of their wooden handles. These were decorated with complex patterns made up of minute gold pins. There was a bronze axe and what may have been a stone-headed sceptre with bone decorations to its handle. But the most spectacular finds were three objects all made of pure gold – a breast plate, a smaller lozenge-shaped sheet (the top object shown on the inside front flap) and a belt hook (the bottom object shown on the inside front flap). This burial from Bush Barrow, dating to about 1800 BC, is the richest in the immediate vicinity of Stonehenge.

The Normanton Down Barrows are privately owned but Bush Barrow and the adjacent disc barrows can be viewed from nearby paths.

Above: A magnificent gold breast plate from Bush Barrow, one of the barrows in the Normanton Down group
Below left: The Normanton Down Barrows. Bush Barrow, where spectacular finds were made in 1808, is to the right of this photograph, crowned with a single bush
Below: A bronze dagger and a bronze axe with the reconstructed sceptre (left) from Bush Barrow. All the finds from Bush Barrow are now in the Wiltshire Museum, Devizes

Wider Landscape

A large area of the landscape around Stonehenge is owned by the National Trust, where open access on foot is permitted. This area is indicated on the map. There are, however, many significant prehistoric sites and groups of sites beyond the open access area. Nine of the most important are featured here. Some of these sites are not now visible on the ground and, as they all lie on private, Ministry of Defence or farmed land, it is not possible to visit without specific permission. All, however, help to reveal the richness of Stonehenge's prehistoric landscape.

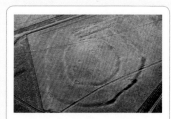

ROBIN HOOD'S BALL

Robin Hood's Ball is an early Neolithic causewayed enclosure lying 2.5 miles (4km) north-west of Stonehenge. Built about 3600 BC, it consists of two concentric circuits of ditch and bank, the ditches dug in a series of short segments separated by causeways. These ditches often contain carefully buried deposits of pottery and animal bones, perhaps the remains of feasts. Some enclosures were defensive, others lived in, but the majority were probably ceremonial. Robin Hood's Ball lies in an Army training area and is not accessible to the public.

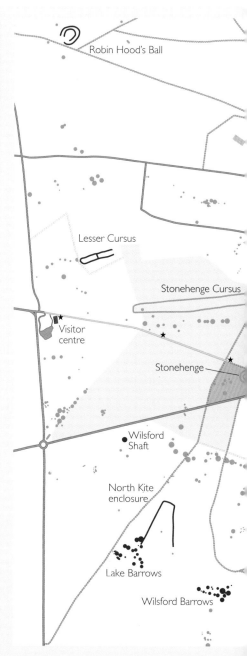

LESSER CURSUS

The Lesser Cursus is much smaller than the Stonehenge Cursus (see page 18), at only about 400m (430yd) long. It was shown by excavations in 1983 to have been only half this length when first built. Strangely, at its eastern end the ditches simply stop, leaving an open end, as if never completed. The newly dug ditches were then quickly filled in, covering a collection of antler picks neatly laid out in a line on one part of the ditch floor. Radiocarbon dates from these picks suggest that the Lesser Cursus was built in about 3500 BC.

WILSFORD SHAFT

The Wilsford Shaft is a 30m (100ft) deep, narrow, circular shaft dug into the chalk at some time between the early Neolithic (about 3500 BC) and the Middle Bronze Age (about 1500 BC). It was discovered and excavated in 1960.

The bottom layers of its filling were waterlogged and preserved organic materials including rope, wool and the remains of wooden buckets. It was originally interpreted as a ritual gateway to the underworld but was more likely to have been a well.

NORTH KITE ENCLOSURE

This three-sided enclosure 1 mile (1.7km) south of Stonehenge originally consisted of a bank with an external ditch enclosing a large area, but open on its southern side. Excavations suggest that it was built in the early Bronze Age although it may simply be part of a system of later Bronze Age boundary ditches. The North Kite lies on private land and cannot be visited, but the earthworks of the west side can be seen from the nearby footpath.

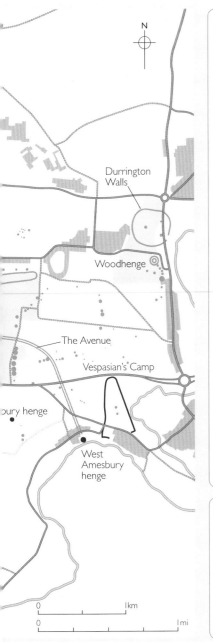

CONEYBURY HENGE

This lies on Coneybury Hill, 0.8 miles (1.4km) to the south-east of Stonehenge. First thought to be a ploughed round barrow, it was shown on aerial photographs to be a small henge, an oval enclosure with a single north-east-facing entrance. This alignment is shared with Stonehenge and Woodhenge. Excavations in 1980 revealed a deep, steep-sided ditch and interior pits containing Grooved Ware pottery. Coneybury was built in about 2700 BC, an early date for a henge monument. It is not visible from ground level, but the site can be viewed from a nearby path.

— Road
— Restricted access road
••••• Byway, bridleway or footpath
----- Permissive path
★ Land train drop-off point
Featured archaeological site
Other archaeological site
Stonehenge ticketed area
National Trust permissive open access land

WEST AMESBURY HENGE

In 2008 Stonehenge's Avenue was found to end, not at the water's edge at the river Avon, but at another small henge. A circular ditch with an external bank enclosed a circle of deep pits. These may originally have contained upright stones, perhaps even some of the bluestones that were eventually set up at Stonehenge. Whatever stood in these pits was removed in about 2500 BC and only then were the ditch and bank of the henge itself built. The site is not visible from ground level and lies on private land.

VESPASIAN'S CAMP

Vespasian's Camp, despite bearing the name of a Roman emperor, is a hillfort of early Iron Age date which lies in a strongly defensive position close to the river Avon near Amesbury. The defences, which in places consist of a ditch and bank, in others

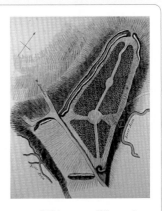

simply a steep scarp, enclose an area of 15 hectares (37 acres). The interior of the hillfort, part of the park of Amesbury House, was landscaped and planted with ornamental trees in the 18th century. The site lies on private land and cannot be visited.

LAKE BARROWS

The Lake Barrows lie on a ridge to the south of Stonehenge, beyond the Normanton Down Barrows. The focus for this cemetery is a large long barrow which lies in woodland just below the crest of the ridge. On all sides of the long

barrow, except to the south-west, lie at least 20 round barrows, including two conjoined disc barrows. These barrows are on private land and cannot be visited, but the Prophet Barrow, which lies just outside the north-west edge of the wood, can be viewed from the nearby footpath.

WILSFORD BARROWS

The Wilsford Barrows lie to the south of Stonehenge on the same ridge as the Lake Barrows. Most notable in this group are the four disc barrows which form the eastern end of the cemetery. These have been largely ploughed flat, although the remaining barrows survive in the adjacent woodland. These barrows lie on private land and cannot be visited.

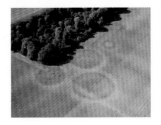

History of Stonehenge

From its earliest phase up to its abandonment some 1,500 years later, Stonehenge was probably the most important temple in Britain. Since then, it has been viewed by different ages and by different people both as an enigma and as a source of inspiration. From the Middle Ages onwards, people have been trying to understand the origins of Stonehenge and answer the fundamental questions about how and why it was built. New excavations and the re-analysis of previous finds have continually changed the way the site and its landscape are interpreted and these changes will continue. So what follows is not the final answer: it is simply our current state of understanding.

Previous interpretations of Stonehenge have divided its long and complex history into distinct stages, or 'phases', which perhaps gives the impression that it was built in this way, as a series of very distinct events. There are certainly times in its history when the appearance of Stonehenge did change dramatically, but in between, there were other subtle alterations which are far more difficult to date with confidence. There are, however, particular moments, snapshots in time, when we do know how Stonehenge appeared. These are described in detail in the following sections: a sacred enclosure; the stone monument; and the altered stones. Together these changes are just part of a process of almost continuous modification of Stonehenge.

BEFORE STONEHENGE

Thousands of years before even the first simple enclosure was built at Stonehenge bands of Mesolithic (Middle Stone Age) hunters set up camp at the edge of the valley of the river Avon, close to the modern town of Amesbury. Perhaps these were the people, the inhabitants of a natural, untamed landscape, who, between 8500 and 7000 BC, raised the great pine totem poles that were found close to Stonehenge. In the valley, a tangle of vegetation and a haven for wildlife, they fished and hunted, subtly modifying the landscape in their search for food.

It would be easy to imagine life at this time as being a struggle for survival in a hostile world but this is far from the case. There were many places, both inland and on the coast, that provided stable supplies of food as well as other necessities such as fresh water, stone for tools, wood for shelter and fuel. In such places, rich with natural resources, it was possible to settle on a more permanent basis.

This was not long after the last ice age had ended in about 10,000 BC, a time when Britain was still connected to mainland Europe. Then as sea levels rose in the warming climate, the vegetation changed and some parts of the new island of Britain became densely forested, with elm, oak and hazel gradually replacing earlier pine forests. But some areas of the chalk remained open, grassy plains that were very attractive to the pioneering farmers of the early Neolithic.

Stonehenge lies within one of these areas, where farming could start without first having to clear woodland with stone axes and fire. These first farmers created small, garden-like fields, unlike those of today, in which they grew cereals such as wheat and barley. Nearby roamed their domesticated animals: cattle, pigs and sheep. These were the people who brought new ideas from mainland Europe: the first simple round-bottomed pottery, new types of flint tools, ground axes and fine leaf-shaped arrowheads, and, most visible today, the idea of building large-scale structures from earth and stone. Farming, even on such a small scale, brings stability. It allows people to come together, to celebrate and to commemorate their dead in ways that demonstrate their ties to the land. These first farmers were the builders of the enclosure at Robin Hood's Ball, of the many long barrows that cluster in this area and of the two cursus monuments that straddle the landscape to the north of Stonehenge. Their imprint changed the Stonehenge landscape, made it special, and laid the foundations for what was to come.

Above: Prehistoric tools from the area around Salisbury Plain, dating from the time of the first Stonehenge, or just before

1 Leaf-shaped flint arrowhead

2 Polished axe

3 Flint scraper for preparing animal hides

4 Flint sickle found in a Neolithic pottery vessel, providing rare evidence of agriculture at this time (now in the Salisbury and South Wiltshire Museum)

Left: Early Neolithic pots with a baggy shape that may imitate the leather vessels more commonly used before this period. These are now in the Wiltshire Museum, Devizes

Facing page: Professor William Gowland (1842–1922, kneeling in the centre) carefully excavating the base of the tallest sarsen in 1901. The workman on the right is sieving soil to recover the smallest finds

A SACRED ENCLOSURE – 3000 BC

The location of Stonehenge may have been influenced both by earlier monuments such as the Stonehenge Cursus and by features visible within the natural landscape, geological gullies and a rare local sarsen boulder, later raised as the Heel Stone.

The first Stonehenge was an earthwork enclosure, its slightly sloping central area defined by an irregularly dug ditch with an interior bank of a more regular profile.

Around parts of the ditch was a small outer, or counterscarp, bank. There were two certain entrances. One faced north-east and remained in use throughout the active life of Stonehenge, while a smaller one faced south. The position of the main,

north-easterly, entrance was crucial to the function of Stonehenge. It faced along the line of the natural gullies towards the midsummer sunrise in one direction and aligned with the midwinter sunset in the other. The alignment of the entrance to the enclosure in this direction was deliberate and suggests that Stonehenge, from its earliest phase, was concerned with the movements of the sun.

The size of the ditch and the volume of material that it would have produced could have formed a bank as much as 2m (6.5ft) high. The irregularity of the ditch suggests that it may have been merely a quarry to provide chalk, the bank being more important. The digging of the ditch can be radiocarbon dated, using samples from antler

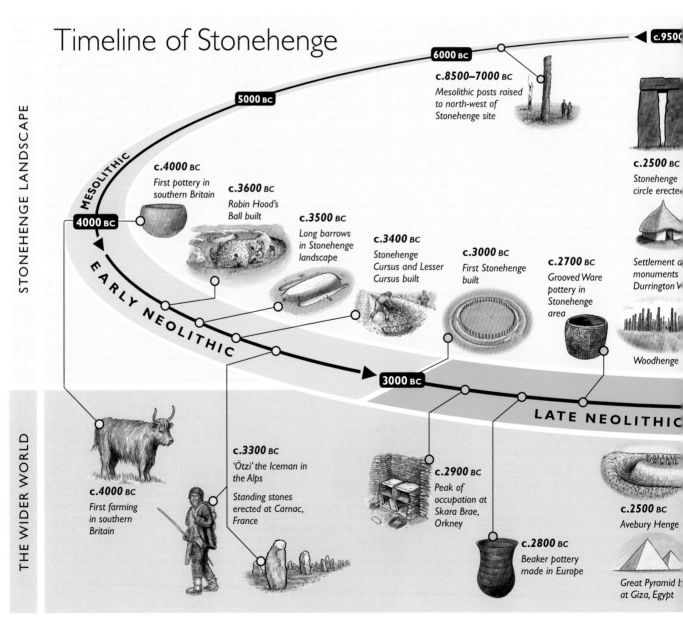

Timeline of Stonehenge

STONEHENGE LANDSCAPE

◄ **c.9500**

6000 BC

c.8500–7000 BC
Mesolithic posts raised to north-west of Stonehenge site

5000 BC

c.2500 BC
Stonehenge circle erected

MESOLITHIC

c.4000 BC
First pottery in southern Britain

c.3600 BC
Robin Hood's Ball built

4000 BC

c.3500 BC
Long barrows in Stonehenge landscape

c.3400 BC
Stonehenge Cursus and Lesser Cursus built

c.3000 BC
First Stonehenge built

c.2700 BC
Grooved Ware pottery in Stonehenge area

Settlement a monuments Durrington V

EARLY NEOLITHIC

Woodhenge

3000 BC

LATE NEOLITHIC

THE WIDER WORLD

c.3300 BC
'Ötzi' the Iceman in the Alps

Standing stones erected at Carnac, France

c.4000 BC
First farming in southern Britain

c.2900 BC
Peak of occupation at Skara Brae, Orkney

c.2500 BC
Avebury Henge

c.2800 BC
Beaker pottery made in Europe

c.2500 BC
Great Pyramid b at Giza, Egypt

picks found on its floor, to about 3000 BC. But cattle bones also from the base of the ditch were found to be as much as 300 years older. These bones, perhaps the relics from ancient ceremonies, suggest that this had been a special place even before the enclosure was built.

The construction of the enclosure was clearly a communal effort and it is possible that individual sections of the ditch were dug by different groups of people. Small bands of individuals, families or tribal groups may have come from some distance to work together on this great project.

Inside the enclosure and around the inner edge of the bank were 56 large regularly spaced pits, the Aubrey Holes, which were dug at the same

time as the ditch. These may have originally held either wooden posts or small upright stones (of bluestone size) but many of them eventually contained deposits of cremated human bone. Many such deposits have been found during excavations, in the partly filled ditch, cut into the bank and just inside its inner edge, as well as in the Aubrey Holes. They are evidence that, very early in its development, Stonehenge was a cemetery. The majority of the cremation deposits were found in the 1920s during extensive excavations by Colonel William Hawley. In 1935, his assistant Robert Newall, without any means of understanding their significance, reburied them in a previously excavated Aubrey Hole.

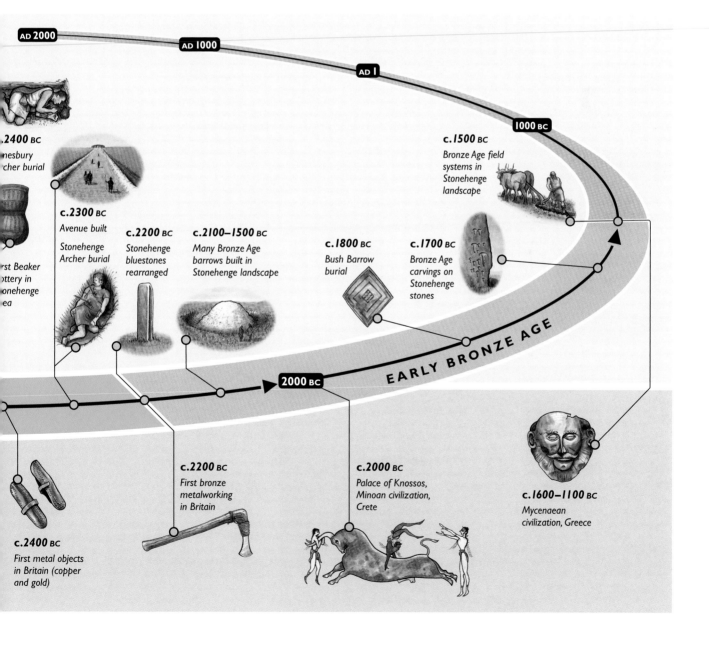

AD 2000

AD 1000

AD 1

1000 BC

c.2400 BC
nesbury
rcher burial

c.1500 BC
Bronze Age field systems in Stonehenge landscape

c.2300 BC
Avenue built

Stonehenge Archer burial

rst Beaker ottery in onehenge ea

c.2200 BC
Stonehenge bluestones rearranged

c.2100–1500 BC
Many Bronze Age barrows built in Stonehenge landscape

c.1800 BC
Bush Barrow burial

c.1700 BC
Bronze Age carvings on Stonehenge stones

EARLY BRONZE AGE

2000 BC

c.2200 BC
First bronze metalworking in Britain

c.2000 BC
Palace of Knossos, Minoan civilization, Crete

c.1600–1100 BC
Mycenaean civilization, Greece

c.2400 BC
First metal objects in Britain (copper and gold)

Right: The ditch and bank were the focus for cremation burials early in Stonehenge's history

Below: A small ceramic dish (top) and a polished ceremonial mace-head (bottom) found buried with cremated human remains in the Aubrey Holes. These are now at the Salisbury and South Wiltshire Museum

Bottom: Reconstruction drawing showing animal bones, some of them hundreds of years old, being placed in the bottom of Stonehenge's newly dug ditch in about 3000 BC

As well as burnt bones many of the cremations found at Stonehenge included ash and charcoal from the funeral pyre. This suggests that the actual process of cremation took place quite close by. Few objects accompany the cremated bones but a number of long pins of antler or animal bone show evidence of having been burnt, presumably along with the body, and may have fastened a shroud. There is also a highly polished stone mace-head, clearly a much-prized possession, and a small ceramic dish possibly used to burn oil or incense.

There is less certainty about what else may have formed part of this first Stonehenge. There may have been larger standing stones in the area around the entrance, the empty holes for which have been found in excavation. In addition, excavations have revealed many smaller holes for upright timber posts, some of which, although undated, may have been raised at this time. In the main entrance to the enclosure and immediately outside were regular rows of small posts and from the second, southern entrance, parallel rows of close-set posts, perhaps part of a fenced entrance passage, wound their way towards the centre of the enclosure. This is the area where it could reasonably be expected that the most important wooden structures would have stood. Unfortunately this is where, in later years, the raising of the stones obliterated the subtle traces of holes for wooden posts. What remains are hints of what may possibly have been a number of small rectangular structures.

This first Stonehenge is an enigma. It was built after the boom in monument construction that produced long barrows, causewayed enclosures such as Robin Hood's Ball and the great cursus monuments. And yet, at this stage, it is not a true henge. There are other cremation cemeteries of this date, but they are rare and they provide the only evidence of burial at this time. The plain pottery vessels of the early Neolithic were being replaced by new decorated styles, including the exuberant Grooved Ware that are such a consistent find in later henges. But houses and villages remain elusive; the landscape seems empty.

THE STONE MONUMENT – 2500 BC

The next stage in the development of Stonehenge saw the start of its transformation, some time about 2500 BC, from a simple earthwork enclosure to something quite spectacularly different. Many stones were brought to the site: huge sarsens from the Marlborough Downs and perhaps elsewhere, and smaller bluestones from the Preseli Hills in Wales.

Immediately outside the enclosure entrance the Heel Stone was probably moved and was joined by two or three entrance stones, one of which still survives as the now recumbent Slaughter Stone. Inside the enclosure four small sarsens, now known as the Station Stones, were set upright just inside the inner edge of the bank. But what radically and permanently changed the appearance of Stonehenge was the arrival, shaping and raising of the 75 sarsens that formed the outer circle and the horseshoe of massive trilithons.

This seems to have happened in about 2500 BC, but over what length of time this major construction took place is unknown. There is also a lack of archaeological evidence to show in which order the two main structures were built. Practicality suggests that the horseshoe of trilithons was built first, or at least before the outer circle was largely finished. What is more certain is that by about 2400 BC, Stonehenge had been transformed. The outer circle was probably complete but varying care had been taken in the way in which it was constructed. The north-east side, facing out towards the entrance, was extremely elegant, the gently curved lintels beautifully shaped and jointed and the upper surface of the stone ring that they formed almost exactly level. Recent detailed studies of the stones, based on a laser survey, have emphasized that the stones on this side of the circle, those that can be seen from the entrance, are much more finely worked and smoothed. In contrast, the south-western side of the circle appears irregular and almost unfinished with many stones far more roughly shaped.

Below: Stonehenge from the Avenue. The ruins of the stone structures that transformed its appearance in about 2500 BC are still hugely impressive

Why Was Stonehenge Built?

This is the most difficult question for archaeology to answer. Stonehenge has no obvious practical purpose. It was not lived in and could not have been defended, so there must have been a spiritual reason why Neolithic and Bronze Age people put so much effort into building it.

Below: The bluestones might have been thought to have had healing powers

Bottom: Midwinter was perhaps the most significant and spiritual time of the year for the builders of Stonehenge

For these people, farmers who were dependent on the success of their crops and animals, winter would have been a time of fear – dark months when days grew shorter and colder and when food supplies grew low. There would have been a longing for the return of the light and warmth that meant crops could grow and animals thrive. Light meant life. This may be a reason why Stonehenge was built and aligned so carefully: to mark the changing seasons and the sun's annual journey around the sky. It marked not the longest day but the shortest, the winter solstice, the turning of the year, after which light and life would return to the world.

But there may be other reasons. Starting early in its long history Stonehenge was a place of the dead where cremated human bones were buried. It has even been suggested that the cold, hard standing stones represented long dead ancestors, in contrast to the wooden structures for the living at nearby Durrington Walls and Woodhenge.

Clues may also lie in the mysterious bluestones, transported all the way from the Preseli Hills in Wales, where there are folk tales told about their healing powers, tales that may have their origins far back in prehistoric times. So a belief in the healing powers of these stones may be one reason why so much effort went into moving them over such a great distance.

These last two reasons may provide the clues as to why Stonehenge was transformed with stones centuries after the first enclosure was dug: the Welsh bluestones brought the promise of healing while the sarsens marked for all time where the ancestors were buried.

Stonehenge can perhaps best be seen as the prehistoric equivalent of a great cathedral, like nearby Salisbury, built for worship but also as a place where believers could come to find healing and hope and where important people could be buried.

But was Stonehenge a place of ceremony at special times of the year? Were the stones decorated with paint or garlanded with flowers? Were there songs and dancing, processions and feasting? These are secrets that Stonehenge still keeps – archaeology cannot provide the answers.

Equally elegant and even more massive were the five sarsen trilithons, graduated in size from the shortest pair that faced each other across the open end of the horseshoe to the tallest, the Great Trilithon, that stood facing the enclosure entrance. This horseshoe re-emphasized the alignment of the whole temple, originally established by the position of the entrance into the earthwork enclosure. The sarsens also show some variation in their selection as each trilithon has one upright that is very well shaped and one that is rougher. This appears to be deliberate but what is its significance? Male and female? Art and nature? We can only guess. The same stones also vary in the degree to which their surfaces have been smoothed and finished. Their inner faces are all flat, while most of the outer surfaces are comparatively rough. The only exception here is the Great Trilithon, the back of which is as smooth as its front.

The sarsens were certainly the most visually impressive element of this transformation of Stonehenge but it seems likely that some of the bluestones, either relocated from the Aubrey Holes or newly arrived from the Preseli Hills, were also set up in the interior at this time. They were not, however, in the locations that they stand in today.

The bluestones were first set up in a peculiar arrangement that is only known from excavation. Two concentric arcs of stone holes, known as the Q and R holes, were found on the northern and eastern sides of the central area of the site. The base of each hole showed the impression of a large stone, in which minute chips of bluestone were sometimes embedded. This setting is difficult to interpret. It does not seem to have been a complete circle as few traces of it have been found on what would have been its southern and western sides. It does, however, reflect the axis of the enclosure as multiple stone holes on its north-eastern side point in this highly significant

Above: Reconstruction drawing showing the raising of the huge stones of the sarsen circle in about 2500 BC. This must have involved considerable preparation and engineering skill
Left: The sole standing upright of the tallest trilithon, its companion lying broken in the foreground

Above: The massive mound of Silbury Hill near Avebury in north Wiltshire

direction. This setting is also likely to have incorporated several miniature bluestone trilithons. The evidence for these comes from lintels (with mortise holes) reused as pillars in later settings and from traces of battered-down tenons on the tops of other bluestone pillars. It is also suggested that the Altar Stone was introduced at this time, placed flat at the foot of the Great Trilithon.

This new, enhanced Stonehenge was the product of huge and organized labour. Its components, gathered from distant places and transported with great effort and organization, show the involvement of communities from far and wide. And it was built at a time where other great monuments were being constructed across Britain from south Dorset to Orkney, Ireland and the Hebrides. In this unprecedented construction

boom, henges, stone circles and massive mounds like Silbury Hill near Avebury, were built by highly organized communities whose characteristic pottery was the highly decorated Grooved Ware. Within the Stonehenge landscape there are other henges: Woodhenge and Coneybury and, at Durrington Walls, not only a great chalk enclosure with massive timber circles but also evidence of everyday life. This may well have been the village of the Stonehenge construction workers, lived in only at certain times of the year and the scene of great feasts to celebrate the changing seasons.

The completion of this stage in the development of Stonehenge marked the end of a massive undertaking for its builders. Their engineering on a monumental scale had created the most iconic prehistoric structure in the world.

The Beaker Culture

Above: A finely potted, elaborately decorated and carefully fired Beaker pot
Right: Reconstruction of a classic Beaker burial – the body is crouched and buried with a Beaker pot, bronze dagger and stone archer's wrist guard

The rebuilding of Stonehenge in stone took place shortly before new ideas, materials and people arrived from the Continent. A new type of finely made and decorated 'Beaker' pottery, a new form of flint arrowhead, new styles of burial and the first use of metals – copper and gold – together characterize this period. From Stonehenge itself and nearby, there are three remarkable human burials which provide a fascinating insight into the great changes that were taking place at this time.

In 1976 an excavation in the Stonehenge ditch revealed a skeleton, buried with finely worked flint arrowheads, some with their tips broken off, and an archer's stone wrist protector. The arrowheads were of Beaker style and the man, who died in about 2300 BC, became known as the Stonehenge Archer.

His bones showed that he was a local, aged about 30, who had met a violent death. The missing tips of the flint arrowheads were embedded in his bones, so the arrows were not possessions but the cause of his death. But even though he died violently, perhaps as a sacrifice, he was given a careful burial in a place that was by that time perhaps the most sacred place in the British Isles.

The discovery in May 2002 of another burial in Amesbury, about 3 miles (5km) from Stonehenge,

provides a stark contrast. The Amesbury Archer, as he became known, had the richest grave ever discovered from the time of Stonehenge. Aged between 35 and 45 years old, he was buried in about 2400 BC with an astonishing collection of rich objects: no fewer than five Beaker pots, three copper knives, two stone wrist protectors, 16 finely worked flint arrowheads and a pair of gold hair ornaments, the earliest gold to be found in Britain. He also had what appears to be a small stone anvil. Analysis of chemicals in his teeth showed that this man was not local, but was born somewhere in the Alps, most probably in what is now Switzerland. So he may have been one of the first to

THE ALTERED STONES – 2200 BC

It might have been thought that the great rebuilding in stone that took place about 2500 BC would have marked the end of Stonehenge's active use. But unlike many other monuments that were built at this time and which mark the end of a Stone Age tradition, Stonehenge continued to be modified and presumably remained important for nearly another 1,000 years. During these years Stonehenge's continuing importance was emphasized by the hundreds of burial mounds that sprung up on every surrounding hilltop.

At Stonehenge some structures did not change. Once in place the massive sarsens, arranged in their circle and trilithons, were never again moved. But centuries later they were decorated. Shallow carvings were added to many of the upright stones, the majority representing broad axe blades that can be dated on the basis of their shape to between 1750 and 1500 BC. They were first noticed in 1953 but recent laser scanning has increased the total to 115, together with three daggers out of six known examples from the whole of Britain (see page 41).

The smaller bluestones were easier to rearrange. By about 2200 BC their first setting, the incomplete circle in the Q and R holes, had been dismantled. Its components, together perhaps with bluestones from other dismantled monuments in the vicinity, were then rearranged as a circle and an oval. The circle, of small unshaped bluestones, lies concentric to and just inside the circle of larger sarsens. The oval, of finely worked pillars, almost all of spotted dolerite, lies inside the sarsen

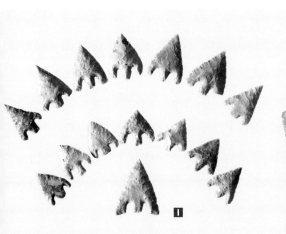

introduce metalworking to Britain, a skill that would have earned him enormous prestige and wealth.

In May 2003 another extraordinary grave was discovered at Boscombe, about 4 miles (6km) from Stonehenge. Dating from about 2300 BC, it contained at least eight Beaker pots, the most ever found in a single grave. But it also contained many skeletons: three adult males, a teenage male and three children aged between two and seven years.

Their skulls suggest that they were all related and some of the bones appeared worn, as if they had been buried previously in another place. Strangely for a Beaker period grave, the method of burial is more like that found in earlier Neolithic long barrows. These men, dubbed the Boscombe Bowmen, were also not local, their teeth showing that some of them had possibly spent the first few years of their lives in Wales, the source of the Stonehenge bluestones, or perhaps in continental Europe.

These three burials from the Beaker period and many others that have recently been analysed using the same scientific techniques show the way that archaeological science can help us to understand the wider cultural influences at work in the building of Stonehenge. At this time, shortly after Stonehenge had been rebuilt in sarsen and bluestone, people were drawn to it from far away in Europe, bringing new ideas which were eagerly taken up by the local population. Both incomers and locals clearly wished to be buried close to Stonehenge, a truly international monument.

Above: Some of the objects buried with the Amesbury Archer (now at the Salisbury and South Wiltshire Museum)

1 A set of fine matched flint arrowheads

2 Copper knives – some of the earliest metal objects found in Britain

3 Gold hair ornaments – some of the earliest objects made of gold in the British Isles

4 Two stone wrist guards

Left: One of the Beaker pots found in the burial of the Boscombe Bowmen

Above: A reconstruction drawing showing how Stonehenge might have looked at sunset on the winter solstice in about 2200 BC

Right: A selection of objects from rich early Bronze Age 'Wessex' burials around Stonehenge

1 Conical shale button with gold cover

2 Pottery 'grape cup' – a type of vessel with applied decoration

3 Miniature amber and gold pendant in the form of an axe

4 Axe-shaped jet bead

5 Spherical gold pendant

6 Spherical shale bead with gold cover

7 Slotted incense cup

8 Bronze daggers

trilithons. This structure, by the removal of a few stones on its north-eastern side, was later turned from an oval into a horseshoe that mirrors the much larger sarsen horseshoe. This then is the final overall arrangement of the central stone structures, the ruins of which can be seen today.

Changes had also taken place in and near to the main enclosure entrance. Stones were removed leaving only the Heel Stone and Slaughter Stone in place. The silted up enclosure ditch itself had been recut, the chalk perhaps used to make the small outer 'counterscarp' bank.

Most obviously, the Avenue was constructed. Following the solstice alignment in its first straight section, the ditches and banks then curved off to the east before swooping down into the valley of the river Avon.

Stonehenge was now complete, the sole final and puzzling addition being two circles of shallow pits, the Y and Z holes, which were dug just outside the sarsen circle perhaps as late as 1600 BC. They do not appear to have held uprights either of stone or timber and were filled with fine wind-blown silt. This soil may well offer

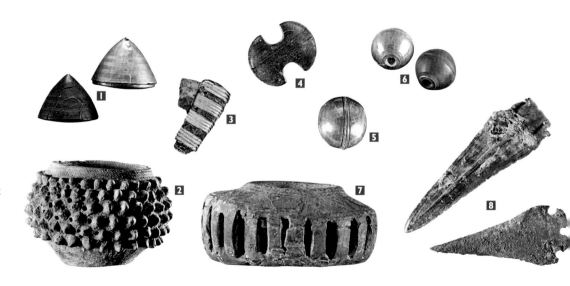

a clue about the end of Stonehenge as a living monument, with the sacred grasslands that surrounded it now ploughed up by Bronze Age farmers.

The importance of Stonehenge in the Beaker period and throughout the early part of the Bronze Age is clearly demonstrated by the cemeteries of round barrows that cluster on every surrounding hilltop. Stonehenge was the magnet, the place to be buried if you were a rich and important person. And this is unusual. Stonehenge was first built and then enhanced in the Neolithic period, by a society that constructed great communal monuments but within which individual people largely remain anonymous. There are no graves of rich individuals from the time when the stone monument at Stonehenge was being built. Those whose burnt remains are buried there must have been important in some way – perhaps priests or architects – but if they had riches then they did not go to the grave with them.

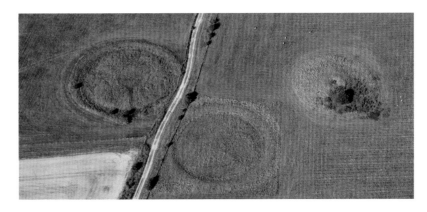

In contrast, those in the later round barrows display their wealth in bronze, gold, jet and amber – so called 'Wessex' burials. They are part of a new society that valued individual power and yet they still chose to be buried close by this ancient relic of a past age. Unlike many other Neolithic monuments around Britain that sunk into obscurity, Stonehenge was a place that obviously still wielded enormous power.

Above: Barrows of the Normanton Down group. Bush Barrow on the right was one of the richest 'Wessex' burials in the Stonehenge landscape

Bronze Age Carvings on the Stones

Ancient carvings on the stones, shallow outlines of a dagger and axe blades, were first spotted by a sharp-eyed archaeologist in 1953. Closer examination of the uprights of the trilithons revealed more axes, so by 2003 a total of 44 had been recorded. These carvings could not be directly dated, but the shapes of the weapons and tools suggest that they date to the earlier part of the Bronze Age, between 1750 and 1500 BC.

More recent studies, including a laser scan of all the stones, have revealed far more carvings, some very shallow and invisible to the naked eye. There are now over 115 axes known, some in complex panels of up to 59 separate carvings, and three definite daggers, out of a total of six known from the whole of Britain. The decoration of Stonehenge, late in its long history, makes it one of the most important sites for prehistoric rock art in Britain: a Bronze Age art gallery.

The link between the daggers and axes found in the rich cemeteries of round barrows that surround Stonehenge, and the outlines of these tools and weapons carved into its hard sarsens, is very clear. It was one more way in which the rich people who lay within the barrows could associate themselves with a site that was already ancient, but which was still enormously important.

Right: The carved outlines of Bronze Age tools on the upright stone of a trilithon represent a dagger with its wooden handle (top) and an axe blade (bottom)

AFTER STONEHENGE

Although building activity at Stonehenge effectively ended by 1600 BC, we have no evidence to show how long after this it continued in use. But even if Stonehenge remained the same, the surrounding landscape continued to change. More and more elaborate round barrows were built, continuing the long tradition of burial around Stonehenge. But from the middle of the Bronze Age (about

Above: A sestertius (large brass coin) of the Roman Emperor Commodus, dating to about 186–7, found during William Gowland's excavations at Stonehenge in 1901
Right: A mid 14th-century manuscript illustration showing Merlin building Stonehenge
Below: Stonehenge drawn by Lucas de Heere, a Dutch traveller, in 1574

1500 BC) there is increasing evidence of everyday life. Boundary ditches were dug, dividing up the landscape, and small, regular fields for cultivating crops spread across land that had formerly been used mainly as pasture. The banks of the Stonehenge Cursus, now more than 2,000 years old, the reason they were built long forgotten, were used as field boundaries by Bronze Age farmers who ploughed its interior. The wind-blown soils that filled Stonehenge's Y and Z holes are evidence of open, cultivated fields nearby. These farmers lived in the small settlements that appeared scattered across the landscape, each a cluster of circular houses of wood and thatch, set within their own collection of fields.

ROMAN AND MEDIEVAL INTEREST

Before the Roman conquest of AD 43, Stonehenge had long ceased to be a living temple but it appears to have had a new lease of life under the Roman invaders. Many finds of Roman date (coins, brooches and pottery) indicate more than just objects dropped by casual visitors; recent excavations have shown that large pits were being dug among the stones and that some bluestones were broken up at this time. What could be regarded as vandalism could have been respect: Stonehenge, like many other ancient sites in Britain, may have been adopted by a new religion and become a Roman shrine.

In about AD 645, a man was buried at Stonehenge. He had been decapitated and may have been executed as a criminal. Sometime after this the name of Stonehenge emerged, formed from the words 'stone' and 'henge', the latter meaning 'hanging' and possibly referring to the gallows-like arrangement of upright stones and their lintels.

From medieval times onwards much energy was expended in trying to guess the date, the builders and the purpose of Stonehenge. The first written description, dating from about 1130, appeared in Henry of Huntingdon's *History of the English People*, where he described 'Stanenges, where stones of wonderful size have been erected after the manner of doorways … no one can conceive how such great stones have been so raised aloft, or why they were built there'.

In 1136 Geoffrey of Monmouth explained in his *History of the Kings of Britain* that Stonehenge was

a memorial to a great battle between Saxons and Britons. He suggested that the stones came from an Irish stone circle called the Giants' Round, transported to Salisbury Plain and magically re-erected there by the wizard Merlin. This idea proved very popular and was widely accepted until as late as the 16th century.

17TH-CENTURY ANTIQUARIANS

Due to a renewed interest in the ancient past during the 17th century, new ways of trying to understand Stonehenge were employed. In the 1620s the Duke of Buckingham had a hole dug in the centre of the monument but was disappointed as it produced nothing more than 'stagges hornes

Above: An engraving of Stonehenge by William Kip from the 1610 edition of William Camden's Britannia. The label 'C' (bottom left) refers to 'the place where men's bones are dug up'

Above: A copy of a contemporary portrait of Inigo Jones by Sir Anthony Van Dyck
Above right: Stonehenge by Inigo Jones, 1725, drawn as he imagined its original geometric design
Right: An elevation of Stonehenge from the north-east, copied by John Aubrey in the 1660s for his Monumenta Britannica from an original drawing by Inigo Jones. Aubrey described Stonehenge as 'one of our English wonders'

and bulls horries and charcoales'. While an archaeologist today would be more than satisfied with such a collection of samples for radiocarbon dating, they were of no interest to the duke who was hoping for something more valuable or spectacular.

King James I (r.1603–25) decided that Stonehenge should be studied in detail and engaged the architect Inigo Jones (1573–1652) to carry out the work. Onto the plan of Stonehenge, Jones superimposed an elaborate geometrical design consisting of four equilateral triangles within a circle. He needed a degree of imagination to do this: an extra trilithon had to be added to create the required perfect symmetry but to Jones it was sufficient proof that Stonehenge must have been built by the more 'civilized' Romans.

The Danes and Phoenicians soon appeared alongside Saxons and Romans as potential builders of Stonehenge, although there were some who

began to suggest that the ancient Britons were responsible. Among these was John Aubrey, a Wiltshire-born antiquary.

He realized that it was a fruitless exercise searching for the builders of Stonehenge in written historical records because such sites were 'so exceeding old that no Bookes doe reach them'. Aubrey produced his first plan of Stonehenge in 1666. It was one of the first accurate drawings of the site ever made and on it he noted a series of 'cavities in the ground' close to the inner edge of the bank. Over 250 years later excavation proved that these depressions marked the position of large pits that were named Aubrey Holes after the man who had noticed them first. Many of Aubrey's ideas are fanciful but he did conclude correctly that Stonehenge was a temple built by the ancient Britons, even though he was among the first to assume wrongly that the priests attending the temple were Druids.

The Druids

It is a commonly held belief that Stonehenge was built by the Druids. This is not the case. Today's Druids are a 19th-century reinvention, but there were real ancient Druids: priests who flourished in the Iron Age, the centuries just before the Roman occupation of Britain in AD 43.

The association between Stonehenge and the Druids is due to the writings of 17th- and 18th-century antiquaries, including William Stukeley.

Stukeley was fascinated by Stonehenge and correctly deduced that it was built not by

the Romans or Danes but by the people who lived in Britain before the Romans arrived. He also recognized it as a temple. Temples need priests and the only

ancient priests Stukeley knew of were the Druids described by Roman writers. So Stukeley's deduction that the Druids had built Stonehenge was

entirely logical but wrong. Even the Iron Age Druids did not in fact emerge until more than 1,000 years after Stonehenge was abandoned.

Above: A late 18th-century engraving by S Sparrow of a Druid near a Stonehenge-like structure. Such depictions were inspired by the writings of William Stukeley and others

18TH- AND 19TH-CENTURY INVESTIGATIONS

John Aubrey's ideas were taken up in the early 18th century by William Stukeley, a Lincolnshire-born doctor and pioneering field archaeologist. He had the great advantage of seeing the downland that surrounded Stonehenge before much of it was ploughed up and was the first to notice not only the Avenue leading up to Stonehenge, but also the Stonehenge Cursus, a long Neolithic earthwork just to the north (see page 18). Stukeley also coined the term 'trilithon' (from the Greek for 'three stones') to describe the arrangement of two uprights capped by a horizontal lintel. Unfortunately, however, Stukeley too became obsessed with the idea of Stonehenge being a Druid temple, and this coloured many of his later observations.

On 3 January 1797 an entire trilithon collapsed. This was the first recorded fall of stones at Stonehenge. Among those who visited at this time

Left: Portrait of William Stukeley by Richard Collins, painted about 1728–9. Stukeley was the first antiquarian to notice and record the Avenue and the Stonehenge Cursus

45

was William Cunnington who went on, with his fellow archaeologist, Sir Richard Colt Hoare, to investigate many of the barrows that surround Stonehenge (see page 24). But although the two men applied increasingly scientific methods to their investigations, Stonehenge remained a mystery. Colt Hoare, in his *Ancient History of Wiltshire*, described it in the following words: 'How grand! How wonderful! How incomprehensible!'

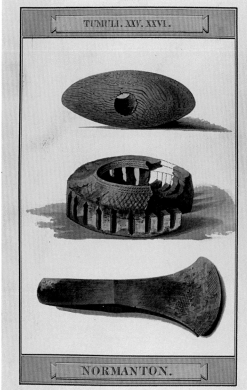

Above: A watercolour by Philip Crocker of William Cunnington and Sir Richard Colt Hoare overseeing barrow diggers at work at Normanton Down, south of Stonehenge, in about 1810

Right: Philip Crocker was Colt Hoare's draughtsman. He made beautiful watercolours recording the finds excavated from the barrows around Stonehenge, such as these objects from the Normanton Down Barrows. His watercolours were later reproduced as engravings in Colt Hoare's The Ancient History of Wiltshire, *1812*

It may have remained incomprehensible, but to many artists of the 18th and 19th centuries Stonehenge was an inspiration. Its rugged stones were the epitome of the picturesque ruin, wild and romantic, and they often placed it not in its rather plain downland setting but in wild and imaginary Druid-inhabited landscapes.

In 1883 Stonehenge was formally recognized as being of national importance, included in the 'schedule', the list of monuments that were supposedly to be protected by the newly introduced Ancient Monuments Protection Act. Unfortunately, this did not offer any real protection and in practical terms nothing changed. Stonehenge remained neglected and crumbling and on 31 December 1900, the last day of the 19th century, another stone fell.

EARLY 20TH CENTURY

The collapse at Stonehenge affected attitudes towards the monument, marking its move not only into the 20th century but from ruin to national treasure. In 1901 there were protests as the owners of the site, the Antrobus family of West Amesbury, fenced Stonehenge off for the first time, introducing an admission charge of one shilling (the equivalent of about £4.50 in today's money). This year also saw the first restoration work.

The sole surviving upright of the Great Trilithon, which had been leaning at a precarious angle, was straightened and firmly bedded in concrete. The engineering work was accompanied by an excavation, carried out to a high standard by

Professor William Gowland. He published his results very promptly, concluding that the stone had first been raised at the very end of the Stone Age or beginning of the Bronze Age, a very accurate interpretation of the evidence.

At this time Stonehenge lay on the Antrobus estate, based nearby at West Amesbury. But in 1915, with Sir Edmund Antrobus dead and his heir killed in action in the First World War, the entire estate was put up for auction. Lot 15 was Stonehenge, sold for £6,600 to Cecil Chubb, a local landowner who apparently bought it on impulse.

Three years later, influenced by the revised and improved Ancient Monuments Act of 1913, Chubb was persuaded to give his impulse buy to the nation and was rewarded with a knighthood.

But in 1919 the condition of Stonehenge was once again causing concern and more restoration was planned, this time on a grander scale. An experienced archaeologist, Colonel William Hawley, was brought in by the Office of Works to work alongside the engineers but he had an additional task: to excavate, on behalf of the Society of Antiquaries of London, the whole of Stonehenge. In 1919 he started work on the sarsen circle where several leaning stones, which for many years had been prevented from falling over by

wooden props, were winched to an upright position before being set in concrete. He continued to dig for the next six years, often working alone, and excavated many of the Aubrey Holes, about half of the ditch and a considerable part of the eastern side of the interior of the enclosure.

But although the restoration had made much of Stonehenge safe once more, the excavations, the results of which were never properly analysed or published, had been far from satisfactory.

Above: View of Stonehenge at the end of the 19th century showing it in a ruinous state, the tallest upright of the Great Trilithon leaning at a precarious angle

Above: In this photograph of 26 October 1918, Sir Alfred Mond, First Commissioner of Works (left), accepts Stonehenge on behalf of the nation from Cecil Chubb (right)
Left: Restoration work on the sarsen circle in 1919: a lintel in the process of being replaced

MODERN INVESTIGATIONS

In 1950 archaeologists returned to Stonehenge. Professors Richard Atkinson and Stuart Piggott and the Wiltshire archaeologist JFS Stone took up the challenge of preparing Hawley's findings for publication but also felt that some additional investigation was needed. They began by excavating two more Aubrey Holes, one of which provided a sample of charcoal for the first radiocarbon date for Stonehenge. The date, sometime between 2123 and 1570 BC, was rather imprecise but marked a real breakthrough. For the first time, Stonehenge had been dated scientifically.

Annual excavations continued until 1958 when another major engineering project began, to raise the entire trilithon that had fallen in 1797. This involved freeing the great fallen stones from the earth and moving them to storage before archaeological excavations could be carried out. Atkinson and his colleagues were able to investigate the shape of the original holes dug to receive the stones, providing important clues about how they had originally been raised. Finally, the replaced uprights were set in a bed of concrete and the lintel was replaced. The trilithon stood once more and the ruins of Stonehenge

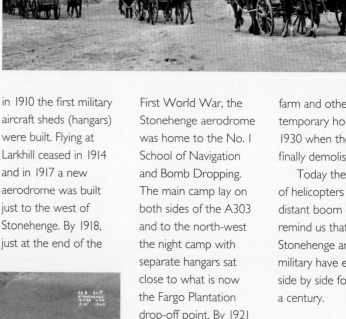

Stonehenge and the Military

In 1897 the British Army started to carry out artillery exercises to the north of Stonehenge, drawn by the relative isolation and the availability of large expanses of cheap farmland. At first soldiers on exercise lived in tents but later, at the time of the First World War (1914–18), huge numbers of more permanent huts were built in the area of what

is now Larkhill Camp. Traces of the military railway which brought troops and supplies into the camp from Amesbury can still be seen on the ground. Larkhill Camp, its tin huts replaced long ago by more permanent buildings, is still the home of the Royal Artillery.

The Stonehenge area was also the scene for pioneering flying. The first planes flew from Larkhill in 1909 and a year later

in 1910 the first military aircraft sheds (hangars) were built. Flying at Larkhill ceased in 1914 and in 1917 a new aerodrome was built just to the west of Stonehenge. By 1918, just at the end of the

First World War, the Stonehenge aerodrome was home to the No. 1 School of Navigation and Bomb Dropping. The main camp lay on both sides of the A303 and to the north-west the night camp with separate hangars sat close to what is now the Fargo Plantation drop-off point. By 1921 it had been closed and in the following year the site was returned to its owner, Isaac Crook (it had been requisitioned for military use). The military buildings were supposed to be dismantled, but some were reused as a pig

farm and others as temporary housing until 1930 when they were finally demolished.

Today the sounds of helicopters and the distant boom of artillery remind us that Stonehenge and the military have existed side by side for over a century.

Above: In 1915, troops of the 10th Battalion Canadian Rifles cross Stonehenge on their way to Larkhill Camp
Left: Aerial view of 1928 showing the few remaining buildings of the Stonehenge aerodrome close to Stonehenge. They were demolished a few years later

were now far easier to understand. Excavations carried on until 1964 but once again, despite the appearance in 1956 of a book by Richard Atkinson simply entitled *Stonehenge*, no scientific reports were written. It was not until 1995 that the results of all the 20th-century excavations were finally analysed and published.

In 2008 two separate excavations were carried out at Stonehenge, the first for over 40 years. Both were small by the standards of previous investigations but highly significant. In May, Professors Timothy Darvill and Geoffrey Wainwright excavated a small trench on the line of the Q and R holes, the enigmatic bluestone setting that was thought then to pre-date the sarsen structures. This excavation did not produce any firm dating evidence for the Q and R holes but instead discovered that bluestones had been broken up and removed during the Roman period, the first clues that Stonehenge was actively used at this time. Radiocarbon dates also showed evidence of Mesolithic activity on the site, from the time that the nearby 'totem poles' were raised (see page 17).

In August 2008, a team led by Professor Mike Parker Pearson re-excavated the cremated human remains first discovered by Colonel Hawley in the early 1920s (see page 33) but reburied in Aubrey Hole 7 in 1935. Unfortunately these had been tipped into the empty Aubrey Hole in a jumbled mess, mixing up cremated human bones from many locations around the site. Despite this it is possible to say that they represent at least 63 individuals,

Above: The restoration of a fallen trilithon in 1958 was a major modern engineering project
Left: Professors Timothy Darvill and Geoffrey Wainwright excavating in 2008; their dig yielded the unexpected evidence that Stonehenge had been used by the Romans

Local Perspectives

Above: Richard Crook photographed on his first birthday with his father Norman (right) and his grandfather Isaac (left)

Richard Crook, a local farmer, recalls his family's part in the sale of Stonehenge, shortly before Cecil Chubb donated the site to the nation:

'Isaac Crook, my grandfather, moved here from down the road in 1908. Isaac farmed Normanton Farm – that's why my father's called Norman. Isaac kept his pigs and horses behind Stonehenge in the Royal Flying Corps hangars.

'In 1915, there was a big sale. Isaac was the underbidder to Stonehenge. He bid £6,500 – and it was sold for £6,600 to a chap by the name of Cecil Chubb.

'By the Sixties, I'd left school and was running riot. One year, the news reported two incidents at Stonehenge: a custodian's cap had been nicked, and one strand of barbed wire was broken – well, I broke that, getting over the fence!

'A gang of us had been to a dance until the small hours and afterwards we went to watch the sun rise at Stonehenge. I then started work at seven. I can remember that 21 June was a hot day that year because the staff stuck my head in a water trough when I went to sleep driving a tractor.

'The best place to see the sun set on Stonehenge is from a neighbouring farm. The farmer's related to me because his son married my daughter. And my other daughter married another farmer round the stones.

'We got the job tied up pretty well. We couldn't buy it, so we married it!'

mostly men but also women and children. A single cremation found close to the edge of the Aubrey Hole was that of a woman, dated to between 3000 and 2910 BC, very early in Stonehenge's history.

As the understanding of Stonehenge changed during the 20th century, so too did its appearance and the way it was managed. Although an admission fee had been charged since 1901, members of the public could wander among the stones for many years after this. In 1963 the interior was gravelled in order to reduce erosion but by 1978 the numbers of visitors had risen so high that it was decided to restrict access to the stones during normal opening hours. The centre was grassed over and the line of an old track through the earthwork enclosure was surfaced, to allow visitors a good view of the stones.

In 1986 Stonehenge was inscribed, along with Avebury, on the prestigious World Heritage List, in recognition of the outstanding prehistoric remains at both sites and in their surrounding landscapes.

STONEHENGE FOR ALL

It has been said that every age has the Stonehenge that it deserves and it is certainly true that over the past centuries Stonehenge has been viewed by successive generations in a wide variety of ways. After the scientific advances of the 19th century, when it was realized that Stonehenge was in fact a product of native Britons, without any exotic influence, the 20th century saw a resurgence of alternative ideas. In a technological age Stonehenge was 'decoded' and seen as a prehistoric computer. For the first time, humans could reach out beyond their own world and so it is hardly surprising that extraterrestrial influences were seen in Stonehenge; suggestions reinforced by the appearance of mysterious crop circles in nearby fields.

In terms of function, Stonehenge has long been regarded as a temple – the prehistoric equivalent of a great cathedral – but it has also been interpreted as a symbol of commemoration for historic battles and an observatory for recording the movements of sun, moon and stars. In an age in which the computer symbolized the height of achievement it was, again, not surprising that Stonehenge was interpreted as an ancient computer: the pattern of its standing stones endowed with hidden meaning and mathematical significance. In recent years, Stonehenge, which had for a time been a focus of conflict centred on the summer solstice, has become a focus for celebration. To many, in an age where there is a resurgence in earth religions and new paganism, Stonehenge is once again a living temple, a place where the ancient seasonal festivals and ancestors can be commemorated. So alongside the modern Druids, who have now had over a century of association with Stonehenge, people of all nations and all beliefs come to celebrate.

Above: In 2008 the excavation of Aubrey Hole 7 recovered the cremated bones that had been redeposited there by Colonel Hawley and his team over 70 years earlier
Below: Summer solstice celebrations in 2010

Above: The reconstructed interior of one of the Neolithic huts. Such archaeological experiments have helped to increase our understanding of the daily lives of the builders of Stonehenge

Below: A frosty sunrise at Stonehenge

RECENT WORK AND THE FUTURE

Our understanding of both Stonehenge and its landscape will continue to improve and change. Twenty-first-century excavations have redated and redefined some familiar monuments as well as making some surprising new discoveries. Extensive geophysical surveys have produced an astonishing array of intriguing new monuments. This well-studied landscape is still capable of producing surprises.

The surroundings of Stonehenge and the ways in which both the monument and the landscape are presented and explained have also changed radically over the past few decades. Cultivated fields have been replaced by restored grassland, monuments have been cleared of tree growth and wider areas have been made accessible to the public. At Stonehenge itself the changes have been even more radical. To the south, Stonehenge is still bordered by the busy A303, all attempts either to divert the road or place it in a tunnel having failed. But to the north, the old A344, which used to run close by the stones and separate them from the Avenue, has been removed and grassed over. A new visitor centre has been built 1.5 miles (2.5km) to the east at the edge of the World Heritage Site providing parking, a shop, a café, educational facilities and exhibitions on Stonehenge and its landscape. From here a land train transports visitors to within walking distance of the stones. This ambitious project has fulfilled the vision for the future of the site outlined in the Stonehenge World Heritage Site Management Plan: to restore the landscape setting and tranquillity of Stonehenge, to improve visitor access to the surrounding monuments and to protect the archaeological landscape of which Stonehenge is such an important part.

So what is Stonehenge in the 21st century? It is certainly an icon, its unique stone settings instantly recognizable as enduring symbols of solidity and ancient achievement. It is a major tourist attraction with more than 1,000,000 visitors a year and also a site of huge archaeological and scientific importance. Centuries of study, excavation and analysis have shown when Stonehenge was built and provided clues to the identity of the builders. As the understanding of people's lives at the time of Stonehenge increases, it also helps to explain why such huge effort was expended by our prehistoric ancestors. But there is much that we still do not know and it is here, in Stonehenge's mystery, that part of its appeal lies. This great temple, the most magnificent prehistoric structure in the whole of Britain and Ireland, will always keep some of its secrets.